...ying

MANCHESTER
1824

Manchester University Press

POCKET POLITICS

SERIES EDITOR: BILL JONES

Pocket politics presents short, pithy summaries of complex topics on socio-political issues both in Britain and overseas. Academically sound, accessible and aimed at the interested general reader, the series will address a subject range including political ideas, economics, society, the machinery of government and international issues. Unusually, perhaps, authors are encouraged, should they choose, to offer their own conclusions rather than strive for mere academic objectivity. The series will provide stimulating intellectual access to the problems of the modern world in a user-friendly format.

Previously published
The Trump revolt   Edward Ashbee
Power in modern Russia: Strategy and mobilisation   Andrew Monaghan
Reform of the House of Lords   Philip Norton

Lobbying
The dark side of politics

Wyn Grant

Manchester University Press

The right of Wyn Grant to be identified as the author of this work has been
asserted by him in accordance with the Copyright, Designs and Patents
Act 1988.

Published by Manchester University Press
Altrincham Street, Manchester M1 7JA

www.manchesteruniversitypress.co.uk

British Library Cataloguing-in-Publication Data
A catalogue record for this book is available from the British Library

ISBN   978 1 5261 2668 9   paperback

First published 2018

The publisher has no responsibility for the persistence or accuracy of URLs for
any external or third-party internet websites referred to in this book, and does
not guarantee that any content on such websites is, or will remain, accurate or
appropriate.

Typeset by
Servis Filmsetting Ltd, Stockport, Cheshire
Printed in Great Britain by
CPI Group (UK) Ltd, Croydon, CR0 4YY

Contents

List of tables

Introduction

Many different terms are used to describe the exercise of influence on political decision-makers. The variety and range of language reflects the controversy that surrounds the activity. Is the act of lobbying, the attempt to exercise such influence, a perversion of the democratic process that promotes the interests of the rich and powerful at the expense of the less well-off and the public interest? Or is it simply an application of the principle of freedom of association that improves the democratic progress by enhancing the range and quality of information available to decision-makers?

The term 'lobbying' derives from the particular location in which the activity supposedly takes place, the parliamentary or legislative lobby. In practice, most lobbying takes place elsewhere: in government offices, in restaurants or online. An alternative term to describe the organisations involved is pressure groups, which could imply that the application of 'pressure' is in some way improper or involves the misuse of sanctions. More positive terminology is found in terms such as 'campaign group', 'altruistic group' or 'advocacy group', although these are usually applied to groups promoting a particular cause rather than lobbies representing sectional interests. The actual terminology used is important in conveying an impression of an organisation. The Council for the Preservation of Rural England rebranded itself as the Campaign to Protect Rural England in 2002 to counter the impression that it was a backward-looking, establishment charity or statutory body. It should also be noted that some cause groups are effectively 'protest businesses', with chequebook or direct debit memberships who have little opportunity to shape the policies of the organisation to which they belong.

More neutral terms are 'interest group', 'stakeholder' and 'non-governmental organisation' (NGO), although the latter term undoubtedly carries more favourable connotations than the former. The term NGO was devised by the United Nations in 1945 to refer to organisations that qualified for its Economic and Social Committee. In its original form it referred to a wide spectrum of organisations that were neither part of the state nor engaged in market activity. Its common use now is to refer to groups that fight for a particular cause such as the protection of the environment or aid to the Global South. It is usual to apply a 'public interest' or benevolence test to their activities.

The Edelman trust survey has shown for many years that there is more public trust in NGOs than in the media, business or government. NGOs are 'consistently seen to be the most trustworthy organisations in society, in survey after survey' (Keating and Thrandardottir, 2017: 141). Individuals who feel an ideological or solidarity connection with an NGO are more likely to perceive it as trustworthy. However, this trust is a fragile resource that needs to be nurtured. 'Issues of NGO trustworthiness came into renewed focus in the 1990s with several publications that questioned whether NGOs were the saviours they claimed to be' (Keating and Thrandardottir, 2017: 135).

'Interest group' may be taken to refer to an organisation that represents a particular section of society, such as an industry, a profession, or a group of workers or farmers. Their function is to look after the common interests of a sector of society and their membership is normally restricted to that sector. 'Stakeholder' is a term used in government, and carries with it the implication that the lobby or cause has a legitimate interest in the topic under discussion. It also avoids some of the more pejorative terms.

The case for lobbying

The freedom to associate is at the heart of liberal democracy and the presence of a vast array of political associations in a country could be seen as a sign of a healthy civil society in which citizens are freely able to express their views. Autocracies either prohibit their citizens from joining associations other than state-approved or organised bodies, or at the very least associations enjoy a perilous existence, with their offices raided or their activists imprisoned.

Democracy goes beyond the act of voting, important though that is. Citizens need opportunities to participate in the political process, to express their views and to share and develop them with others. It should be noted that most political organisations offer relatively limited opportunities for democratic citizenship. In many 'protest businesses', internal democracy is very limited. Greenpeace, for example, is a hierarchical organisation that has 'supporters' rather than 'members'. 'The purpose of the Greenpeace supporter was not so much to reflect on the nature of the problem, but to take action in promoting a solution which had already been set out by the NGO itself' (Hilton et al., 2013: 21).

Such 'followership' organisations were not welcome to those who saw campaigning organisations as part of a solution to declining democratic engagement. 'There is a concern that groups – and the group system in aggregate – are becoming less capable as democratic actors in their own right' (Halpin, 2014: 8). It has been argued that early twentieth-century groups were often based on branch structures and membership engagement, but such groups are now the exception rather than the rule. Professional staffs have taken over and memberships are there to provide financial support and at best to be mobilised rather than to participate.

That is not to say that members are dissatisfied with a passive support as distinct from an active engagement model. Even when opportunities are provided to vote on the organisation's leadership or policies, the majority of members generally do not take them up. Apart from the Automobile Association, which is really a commercial service organisation, the National Trust is the largest mass membership organisation in Britain, with over four million members. Members can vote online or by post, but only around 25,000 voted on resolutions at the 2016 annual general meeting, with the most successful candidate for election to the council receiving just under 17,000 votes. The vast majority of members join to gain access to the Trust's properties rather than to shape its conservation policies.

Nevertheless, representative organisations take democracy beyond a simple head-counting exercise to reflect the intensity of views held by citizens. They provide an additional route for political participation, allowing citizens to develop political skills that may be applied elsewhere in the political process. Hence they are a source of social capital. They may encourage citizens to feel that they are fully involved in the political process and that it is responsive to them. They may therefore counter political exclusion, particularly at a time when more conventional forms of political involvement are declining. They allow a diversity of opinions to be expressed, which is important in a more fragmented society, and they facilitate views that are more 'fine grained' than those expressed by political parties. They also offer a chance for minority and disadvantaged groups to argue their case. This addresses a tension at the heart of democratic government. Democracy is a majoritarian form of government, but it also aspires to protect minority rights.

It should also be noted that the internal democracy test is not necessarily an appropriate one to apply to a lobbying group. Halpin has argued that internal democratic structures are not achievable when an NGO's principal concern is with solidarity, advocating on behalf of non-human constituencies such as animals or concerned with the fate of future generations with regard to such issues as climate change. They may resort to claims based on evidence or moral authority rather than membership endorsement of their policies. Not all groups are capable of representation. There is a tension between democratisation projects and those concerned with tackling political exclusion.

An insistence on 'internal democracy and participation as a pre-requisite to access would simply remove a large number of NGOs from formalised political forums' (Halpin, 2009: 76).

Lobbies can provide information which can improve the quality of decision-making. Britain has a generalist civil service, and although it has some specialists, they are often stretched in terms of their ability to contribute to decision-making. Moreover, there are some topics on which even the specialists will not be well informed. Lobbying organisations may have a better understanding of these issues, or at least be able to obtain the necessary information from their members. They can simplify the policy task by reducing uncertainty and helping to define what the key issues are. This process of issue definition is, of itself, a means of exerting influence.

It could be argued that there is an incentive for lobbies to distort such information, or at least to present it in a selective or partial way that serves the interests of their members. That is always a risk. However, it should be remembered that lobbying is usually a 'repeated game'. Lobbyists will be engaging with decision-makers on a variety of issues in the longer run. If they provide inaccurate or incomplete information to decision-makers, their reputation will be damaged and they will lose credibility and the trust of those they are seeking to influence.

As well as helping with the design of policies, lobbies can help to secure their effective implementation. In part this is a question of what might or might not work. For example, what sorts of incentives and penalties would encourage firms to provide more training for their workers? Sectoral organisations can also encourage their members to implement government policies, for example by staging joint events to explain the policies and how they might be beneficial.

Groups can create and maintain private regulatory regimes which involve systems of private accreditation, for example certifying foods as organic (the Soil Association) or as meeting animal welfare standards (the RSPCA). Government is then relieved of the cost and effort of creating such regimes itself and, if anything goes wrong, the blame attaches to the body organising them. However, privatised regulation can be less transparent and accountable.

The case against lobbying

The case against lobbying rests on the contention that it creates or reinforces biases in the polity, in particular by ensuring that some interests are more effectively represented than others, or even that some are not represented at all. As Cave and Rowell argue (2015: 9), 'Commercial lobbyists acting for particular, narrow interests bend our system of government to their will to such an extent that it can be said to no longer serve the interests of the wider public.'

The rebuttal of this critique of lobbying was provided by pluralist thinkers, in particular David B. Truman (1951) in his book *The Governmental Process*. One of his objectives was to 'detoxify' interest groups and to show that they were not a threat to the stability and survival of representative democracy. Two concepts were central to his analysis. These are, first, the notion of multiple or overlapping membership and, second, the function of unorganised interests, or potential interest groups (Truman, 1951: 508). It was these concepts that he saw as central to the compatibility of interest group activity with representative democracy, and hence as a principal means of rebutting the more pathological accounts of 'the lobby'. For Truman it was 'multiple memberships in potential groups based on widely held and accepted interests that serve as a balance wheel in a political system like that of the United States' (Truman, 1951: 514).

Truman was forced to admit that even in the United States there were limits to the pattern of overlapping memberships. This made the concept of potential groups and the way in which one interest would be 'countervailed' by another, for example, business by organised labour, even more important. This aspect of his work was systematically criticised by Mancur Olson (1965). Olson is scathing about the assumption that interests simply organise spontaneously when the need arises. Truman and the other pluralists overlook the free rider problem:

> They must show *why* the individual member of the large, latent group will voluntarily support the group goal when his support will not in any case be decisive in seeing that the group goal is achieved, and when he would be as likely to get the benefits from the attainment of that goal whether he had worked for its attainment or not. (Olson, 1965: 129)

Critics of lobbying have been particularly concerned about what they see as the excessive influence of corporate business interests, particularly large multinational companies which may have their own government relations divisions lobbying on their behalf, as well as being active in a variety of business associations. Truman is in greater difficulty in terms of his account of the role of business interests in a democratic polity. His perspective admitted that business was a privileged interest but that this position had been earned through its contribution to the prosperity of American society. Olson and Lindblom have subsequently argued that there are structural and systemic reasons why business is an interest like no other. It should be noted that their arguments were advanced before the onset of globalisation, which has further strengthened the position of multinational companies in relation to national governments.

Lindblom's critique was particularly influential because he was writing from within the pluralist tradition. His analysis was based 'on the absolute dependence of governments for their popularity and legitimacy on economic success, and their perception that they depended for that success on the business community' (Crouch, 2010: 155). Lindblom argued that business executives did not have to pressure, bribe or coerce governments to respect their policy preferences. He believed that fundamental issues such as private property and enterprise autonomy are kept off the political agenda, with disagreements between government and business being confined to secondary issues such as the particulars of regulation.

More generally, there is an issue about the power of concentrated versus diffuse interests. Consider the position of farmers in relation to consumers and taxpayers. Farmers have a strong sense of identity as farmers. This has helped to make the National Farmers' Union (NFU) one of the most effective lobbying organisations in England and Wales (there are separate organisations for Scotland and Northern Ireland). Farmers have benefited from substantial subsidies and tariff protection, which has imposed costs on taxpayers and on consumers in the form of higher food prices. However, taxpayers are likely to be unaware of how much of their taxes are spent on farm subsidies, and consumers are unlikely to be unaware of how prices in the shops are affected. The benefits to farmers are concentrated on one group, while the costs to taxpayers and consumers are diffused over a large number of people.

Very broad interests like those of consumers and taxpayers are very difficult to organise. They are in reality very heterogeneous groups with different priorities and interests. Taxpayers pay different amounts of tax. Some of them may accept taxation as the price to be paid for public services; others may resent the level of taxation and prefer more limited forms of government. Young, single people are often quite heavily taxed, but consume relatively little in the way of public services. Consumers may vary considerably in their levels of risk averseness and how much time they are prepared to invest in comparing alternative products.

The Consumers' Association in the UK has effectively proceeded through a business model in which its traded services pay for its advocacy work. Subscribers pay for access to its magazine *Which?* and other services. It has been able to build up an impressive membership of 573,000, but this is a small fraction of all consumers in the UK. What an organisation such as the Consumers' Association stands for is clear enough. However, what lies behind organisations representing specific segments of consumers is sometimes less clear. On the face of it, organisations that represent patients suffering from medical conditions are there to raise awareness of the condition and encourage research into new treatments. Many of these organisations receive funding from pharmaceutical companies. They can be very effective advocates for the use or wider adoption of expensive drugs.

In the United States use has been made of 'astroturf' organisations, which are bodies that appear to be independent and often have words such as 'citizen' in their title, but in fact have been set up and funded on behalf of particular commercial interests such as those in the pharmaceutical industry. This practice has been less common in the UK, but has been spreading from the United States. The pharmaceutical company Roche employed Weber Shandwick to run a campaign to increase government expenditure on cancer drugs. The resultant body, Cancer United, claimed to represent a coalition of healthcare professionals, but 'there was no mention of it being entirely funded by Roche' (Cave and Rowell, 2015: 137). What this points to is the need for transparency in relation to the activities of lobbying organisations.

Particularly difficult to trace are the 'hidden bargains', where there has not necessarily been interaction between lobbyists and government, but where there is an unspoken understanding of how they might mutually benefit. Government does not have to be actively lobbied to recognise the importance of protecting the interests of the financial services industry in, for example, the Brexit negotiations. It is aware of the contribution that the sector makes to taxation, to employment and to GDP. That does not mean, of course, that lobbying does not take place, particularly when a sector is vulnerable. '[The] large number of meetings ministers held with the representatives of banks between 2010 and 2015 may be a measure not of their political strength but of their vulnerability' (Dommett, Hindmoor and Wood, 2017: 390). However, in those meetings, banks were able to draw on shared understandings of their importance to the UK economy.

Government's relations with the retail sector provide a classic example of this form of 'hidden bargain'. Britain has a highly concentrated food retail sector. There has been a shift of power down the food chain from the farmer and food processor to the retailer. Using their market power, the large multiple retailers have been able to impose increasingly demanding conditions on manufacturers and primary producers, squeezing their margins. The producers have in turn complained through their representative organisations about various retailer practices such as contributing to the cost of new store openings or paying for favourable placement of their goods in store. The government did create a supermarket ombudsman in response, but with relatively limited powers. The competition for market share between large retailers helps to hold down prices. This in turn restrains inflation and in particular reduces its impact on lower-income families, a key area of concern for governments. It does not suit the interests of government to restrain the market power of supermarkets too much.

Conclusions: implications for democracy

The expansion and greater sophistication of lobbying makes the task of government more difficult. Lobbyists make demands of government, but they do not provide solutions. They ask for more funding for a particular activity or request new regulations. They do not have to consider the opportunity cost of their requests. For example, a patient group is likely to get a sympathetic hearing from the media when it requests more funding to treat a particular condition. It does not have to say where that funding should come from.

One solution that was advanced in the past was to incorporate pressure groups into the business of government, particularly the major economic interest groups such as the Confederation of British Industry and the Trades Union Congress. This approach had its heyday in the 1970s under the Heath and Wilson governments and was referred to as 'tripartism' or 'neo-corporatism'. It reflected a time when government was more interventionist in the economy, particularly in terms of prices and incomes policies, which required the consent and active cooperation of organised employers and trade unions. This form of cooperation did not survive under the Thatcher government, which was less interventionist and was suspicious of such arrangements. In any case, the tripartite partners had difficulty in delivering the cooperation of their members.

Political parties traditionally performed the function of aggregating a range of demands from society and deciding on priorities in the face of limited resources. However, even given a revival in the membership of the Labour Party, pressure group memberships far outweigh those of political parties. The Royal Society for the Protection of Birds (RSPB), with 1.2 million members, has more members than all the political parties combined. It has also made a considerable investment in public policy issues, with a staff of around 45 in the public policy area, far more than the much larger National Trust. This investment paid off for the RSPB in securing 31 meetings with senior ministers during the lifetime of the Coalition government from 2010 to 2015, although the National Trust managed 25 such meetings.

Government cannot satisfy all the demands made by lobbyists, but it may seem to be particularly susceptible to those made by corporate interests. This can undermine citizen confidence in the capacity of government and hence in the democratic process.

2

Who are the lobbyists?

THE composition of the universe of lobbying activity has changed considerably since the end of the Second World War. Lobbying is a centuries-old activity, but the greater engagement of the government in the economy after the war enhanced the importance of the producer organisations representing employers and labour. The creation of the National Health Service gave a new role to the British Medical Association (BMA), while the 1947 Agriculture Act made the National Farmers' Union a formal partner with government. Politics in the earlier post-war period was essentially about production. The war-ravaged economy needed to be revived to meet the basic needs of the population and to try and make it internationally competitive. At the centre of politics was a struggle between management and labour over the sharing out of the fruits of production.

Cause groups did exist, but they were not the mass membership organisations that we know today, making use of a combination of evidence-based lobbying, the mass media and various forms of protest. They often relied on connections of various kinds with the political establishment. The Council for the Preservation of Rural England, as it was then called, was 'predominantly a metropolitan-centred movement comprising a small but influential group of intellectuals, members of the artistic and literary establishments and the landed aristocracy' (Lowe at al., 1986: 12). It was able to draw on a particular and deeply culturally embedded understanding of 'Englishness' which revered country landscapes and traditional villages.

'CPRE's "insider" status was not only measured by its ability to speak the language of policy makers; post war legislation also incorporated many of the aspirations held by the organisation' (Lowe, Murdoch and Norton, 2001: 6–7).

The Abortion Law Reform Association (ALRA) challenged existing legislation. It was an organisation that drew on doctors and middle-class women. It had fewer than two hundred members in the early 1960s. It girded itself 'in the armour of the reputations of the great and the good ... The legitimacy of ALRA was secured in its association with a respectable establishment' (Brooke, 2009: 82). The Howard League for Penal Reform drew on those with some association with the criminal justice system such as magistrates, probation officers and prison visitors.

Saunders (2009) has traced how aid and development organisations went through a series of phases. Initially, they were concerned with providing famine relief for victims of war. In a second phase in the 1950s and 1960s there was an increasing emphasis on developing countries. A third phase in the 1960s saw the emergence of political campaigning. The 1970s and 1980s saw lobbying on the political nature of poverty, although charity law proved to be a constraint. A fifth phase from the 1990s saw the development of high-profile campaign coalitions. After 1995 charities were permitted to campaign, provided that this helped them to achieve their charitable aims.

Conservationist organisations have a long history in Britain, with a number being founded in the nineteenth century, but it was in the 1970s that a mass environmental movement developed. The launch of the World Wildlife Fund (WWF) in 1961 can be seen as the bridge between the older and newer type of organisation. While it was an elite initiative with royal patronage to raise funds for wildlife conservation, 'it employed mass media to broadcast its message' (Rootes, 2009: 208). Friends of the Earth was established in Britain in 1971 and Greenpeace in 1977. The membership of the RSPB increased fourfold in the 1970s to 441,000 in 1981. WWF increased its membership fivefold to 60,000 over the decade, while there were 30,000 supporters of Greenpeace.

In other policy spheres, Amnesty International was set up in 1961; Child Poverty Action Group in 1966; Shelter, the homeless campaign, in 1966; and the Campaign for Homosexual Equality in 1969. How can one explain this growth of new forms of cause groups? In broad terms it was a case of the political system catching up with broader socio-economic changes. What one may loosely term the 'Keynesian welfare state' had delivered on its promises. There was full employment and the range and quality of public services had improved. There were still major economic policy issues, but a space had been opened up for a new 'politics of collective consumption'. Rather than being concerned with the outcomes of the production process, it focused on the negative externalities of that process. At its core is a concern with collective goods, or at least goods which have some of the characteristics of public goods. Examples would include the quality of the air we breathe or the quality of the seawater we bathe in.

As their basic needs were satisfied, citizens turned away from 'the now-gratified material needs of work, diet and housing to, instead, the exploration of personal identity and belief as a path to fulfilment' (McKay and Hilton, 2009: 5). The growth of higher education helped to underpin the growth of mass membership cause groups: 56 per cent of long-term members of Friends of the Earth and 53 per cent of members of Amnesty International had a degree (Jordan and Maloney, 1996: 672). Higher education encouraged its recipients to question existing policies; it gave them the tools to develop policy alternatives and mobilise around them, and the confidence to question established elites. However, one must not underestimate the growing sophistication of the groups themselves in using techniques such as mass mailing to attract new members and financial support.

Insider groups and outsider groups

One way of thinking about the range of lobbies is to classify them as 'insider' or 'outsider' groups. Access to decision-makers is a necessary if not a sufficient condition of exercising influence, and insider groups enjoy such access. However, they pay a price in terms of accepting informal 'rules of the game' about the kinds of lobbying techniques that they deploy. A lobby has to be able to demonstrate that it has certain political skills before it can be accepted as an insider group. It has to show that it knows how to present an evidence-based case and accept the outcome of the bargaining process.

The original typology (Grant, 1978) has been further modified to make a distinction between 'core' and 'peripheral' or 'niche' insider groups. The former enjoy continuous access to government, often at the very highest levels, and are consulted on a wide range of issues. The latter are often focused on one government department and are consulted on much more specific issues. It is relatively easy for a group to acquire limited insider status in the sense of being placed on a consultation list, although many such groups will have only a marginal influence on policy formation, or their influence will be confined to a very restricted area.

Outsider groups may be divided into those that are outside 'by necessity' and those that are outside 'by choice'. Outsider groups by necessity lack the political skills to lobby effectively; outsider groups by choice wish to remain outside the political system. They resort to direct action of various kinds, often with the objective not so much of influencing government policy as preventing a particular activity from going ahead: for example, the construction of a road; the planting of GM crops; the culling of badgers in an effort to curb bovine TB; drilling for fracking. The resort to tactics is often the result of a perceived lack of influence as much as ideological preference. It is no surprise that insider groups far outnumber outsider groups (Page, 1999).

One misconception has developed about the original typology. It was never argued that insider status was incompatible with mass media campaigning. A distinction was made between 'low-profile' and 'high-profile' insider groups, with the use made of the media being the distinguishing factor. 'In its most extreme form, the "low profile" strategy would involve concentrating entirely on contacts with government and not making even routine statements to the mass media. A "high profile" strategy involves a considerable emphasis on cultivating public opinion to reinforce contacts with government' (Grant, 2000: 412–13). Lobbyists have to be careful about how they use such tactics. In 2017 business lobbies seeking to influence Downing Street were advised that they had to follow some unwritten rules, 'to tread a careful line, expressing their views only in private meetings rather than through public campaigns'. Officials made it clear that 'any critical statements in the media about immigration, trade or the rights of EU residents will be punished with an immediate cessation of access' (Parker, 2017: 3).

The numbers of the population who are willing to engage in various forms of direct action are small in percentage terms, but still significant in absolute terms. The most systematic data suggests that direct action involves less than one in twenty of all citizens, and this number diminishes further when one looks at various forms of illegal protest such as breaking into research laboratories or occupying construction sites to prevent road building. 'The latter involved less than one per cent of the population in 2002, which is a small number in relative terms but quite a large number in absolute terms' (Whiteley, 2012: 35–6).

Although the insider–outsider typology explicitly avoided a link between insider status and effectiveness in exercising influence, the implicit message was that an insider strategy was more likely to be successful. However, outsider activity has been able to score some successes. In 1990 riots against the poll tax in Trafalgar Square 'transformed the poll tax controversy' (Butler, Adonis and Travers, 1994: 154). The government attempted to demonise the protesters, but public opinion was so hostile to the tax that these efforts were unsuccessful. A campaign of civil disobedience in terms of refusing to pay the tax gathered momentum, with large amounts of tax never collected. The government's decision to eventually replace the tax with a council tax, and to ditch Margaret Thatcher as prime minister, was as much influenced by electoral setbacks as it was by popular protests, but they undoubtedly played their part. Similarly, in

September 2000 a protest by road hauliers and farmers against the price of fuel nearly brought the country to a standstill. Ever since then, governments have been very reluctant to increase fuel tax.

Celebrities, particularly those viewed as 'national treasures', can lend their status to effective campaigns. In 2008 Joanna Lumley became the public face of a campaign to grant Gurkha veterans who had served in the army before 1997 the right to settle in Britain. Those who had served after 1997 had already been granted permission, but the UK government had not extended the offer to all the Gurkhas, who are natives of Nepal. On 20 November 2008 Lumley led a large all-party group, including Gurkhas, on a march from Parliament Square to Downing Street with a petition signed by 250,000 people. She subsequently secured a meeting with the prime minister, Gordon Brown, and a change of policy. However, the experience of the Gurkhas who subsequently settled in the UK has been far from happy, which suggests that such hasty campaigns may not always benefit those they are intended to help.

The development of the internet also reduced the costs of forming new campaigning groups. Someone with a laptop and basic IT skills could launch a campaign from their home. Social media such as Facebook and Twitter helped to spread the message and mobilise supporters. However, there are limits to the influence exerted by such campaigns, as will be discussed in more detail later.

Because much of this campaigning activity takes place in full public view, it is easy to overestimate its influence. Trending on Twitter, air time on television and radio or column inches in the press should not be equated with the actual exercise of influence. It may help to get an issue on to the political agenda, but keeping it there for the time that is necessary to bring about lasting change is more difficult.

Dramatic successes in particular public campaigns can obscure the continuous, behind-the-scenes influence being exercised by established lobbies. Data on the type of lobbyists meeting with government ministers from April to June 2014 found that nearly 50 per cent of meetings were with companies, 1,347 meetings in total; 20 per cent of meetings (535) were with NGOs; 8 per cent (224) were with municipal or state bodies; and 7 per cent (193) were with trade associations. Of the ten most frequent ministerial visitors, seven were listed in the FTSE 100: HSBC (22 meetings), British Telecom (22 meetings), Barclays (19 meetings), BAE Systems (18 meetings), BP (16 meetings), Shell (15 meetings) and AstraZeneca (13 meetings). The leading business lobby, the Confederation of British Industry, had 24 meetings. All this points to the extent to which Britain is a 'company state', in which some of the most important meetings are direct ones between government ministers and leading companies.

These patterns are confirmed by an examination of 6,292 meetings between senior ministers and outside interests during the lifetime of the Coalition government from 2010 to 2015. Nearly 45 per cent of all the meetings held by senior ministers were with business organisations and 'The CBI attended more meetings [158] than any other organisation and held meetings with every single senior minister apart from the Secretary of State for Health' (Dommett, Hindmoor and Wood, 2017: 396). BAE Systems was the company holding the largest number of meetings (78), followed by British Telecom (58).

Businesses are able to talk directly to the very highest levels of government. David Cameron as prime minister had a business advisory group which met once a quarter and had twenty members from Britain's biggest businesses. This was described as 'a small group of business leaders from sectors of strategic importance to the UK'. It was said to 'provide high level advice to the Prime Minister and senior ministers on critical business and economic issues facing the UK. The group will provide a forum to debate the concerns and priorities facing the economy in general, and strategically important sectors in particular' (Business Advisory Group, 2017). Theresa May abolished the group and was less willing to meet face-to-face with business leaders, although she did meet with the chief executive of Nissan over its post-Brexit investment plans. By April 2017 she had held four 'business engagement dinners' with chief executives of leading companies, although lobbying on these occasions is not permitted. Regular contacts were being made through two members of the Downing Street staff: Chris Brannigan, director of government relations, and Jimmy McLoughlin.

Why business is a strong lobby

Pluralist theorists thought that the power of any lobby would be checked by the emergence of 'countervailing' lobbies with an opposing point of view. For a long time it was possible to argue that business was countervailed by trade unions, with the leveraging power of their withdrawal of labour and their political links with social democratic parties. The opposition that business now faces is far more fragmented and potentially less effective. '[The] fragmentation of political action into a mass of causes and lobbies provides systematic advantages to the rich and powerful far more than did a more party-dominated politics, where parties stood for relatively clear social constituencies' (Crouch, 2004: 111). For businesses, lobbying is an investment that can bring financial returns. This is particularly the case for businesses seeking to secure government contracts in the defence industries, construction and healthcare services.

Within the range of business lobbies, those representing industries made up predominantly of large multinational firms and mature, established industries have something of an advantage. Long-established industries generally have good internal networks, established networks of contacts, substantial resources, accumulated expertise and reputational advantages. These advantages develop over time. Olson argues (1982: 78) that, 'with age British society has acquired so many strong organisations and collusions that it suffers from an institutional sclerosis that slows its adaptation to changing circumstances and technologies'. It is more challenging for newer, innovative industries in which small firms predominate to establish effective representative organisations. For example, the companies that develop and market biological pest control agents are, with a few exceptions, generally very small 'start-up' companies, with limited understanding of the political process and few spare resources to devote to lobbying. Conventional agrochemicals are made by multinational chemical companies that have well-resourced lobbies and see bio-pesticides as a potential encroachment on their market.

New industries have to define and establish a distinct identity and this may be complicated by commercial rivalries between innovative technologies. There are a number of associations in the renewable energy sector. The Renewable Energy Association, founded in 2001, claims to cover electric power, heat, combined heat and power, biomethane and, following the acquisition of another association, compost. RenewableUK was formed as the British Wind Energy Association in 1978 and covers offshore and onshore wind and also wave and tidal energy. The Solar Trade Association looks after solar heat and power. There is also an Electricity Storage Network, while there is a separate association for Scottish Renewables which covers all sectors including hydro power. When pushing, for example, for a 'greener' energy strategy, these organisations have to find ways of working together.

There is a marked contrast between this dissipation of effort and lack of unity and the activities of the alcohol industry. There is a long tradition of involvement of the industry in politics. This is an industry in which large multinational corporations play a major role and which is well endowed with financial resources. Some companies also produce and market tobacco and the lessons they have learned from defending smoking appear to have shaped their influence strategies. Alcohol consumption, particularly given its addictive nature, has become a major concern for public health experts in recent years. The industry fears similar restrictions to those imposed on the tobacco industry and wants to be able to continue to market its products as it sees fit. The industry's preference is for self-regulation and partnership with government rather than legislative intervention. It argues that responsibility for reducing the harm associated with alcohol should rest with the individual drinker rather than the industry or society more generally. For government there is a concern that falls in consumption might hit tax revenues or the 'night-time' economy. While curbing alcohol sales could cut tax receipts, depending on the precise formula, it should also lead to a reduction in spending by the NHS. However, these benefits would accrue in the longer run and government's focus tends to be more short term.

The alcohol industry has deployed the whole range of lobbying tactics to considerable effect.

> Tactics have included the use of contract lobbyists; campaign contributions to legislators and political parties; the provision of gifts, honoraria, corporate hospitality and charitable donations; direct links with the executive and legislative levels of government; alliances with other interest groups; the use of front groups; the creation of corporate social responsibility initiatives; and attempts to undermine the scientific evidence on alcohol and health. (Hawkins, Holden and McCambridge, 2012: 301)

As a consequence, policies tend not to reflect the views of public health practitioners. 'What is remarkable is that current UK alcohol policies are far closer to policies advocated by the alcohol industry than those indicated by the prevailing evidence base' (Hawkins, Holden and McCambridge, 2012: 301).

Commercial lobbyists

Commercial or contract lobbyists attract particular concern. They are particularly used by big businesses, which can afford their substantial fees, giving such businesses another advantage in the lobbying game. There are also concerns that their activities lack transparency and are insufficiently regulated. They have been accused of 'a selective approach to the truth, media manipulation, the undermining of opponents and other dubious practices' (Cave and Rowell, 2015: x). Some of them have been formed, at least in part, by former politicians or political advisers, or they employ the relatives of politicians. There have been a number of scandals in which peers and MPs have been caught accepting money in 'sting' operations, or lobbyists have been recorded boasting of the extent to which they can affect decision-making (BBC, 2013). In September 2017 Bell Pottinger was expelled from the Public Relations and Communications Association for stoking racial tensions in South Africa in the course of its representative work. The subsequent loss of major clients and senior staff led the London branches of the firm to appoint administrators. For their part, lobbyists would argue that they seek to adhere to professional practices and codes of conduct, and that one should not generalise from particular instances of unethical conduct.

The first recognised commercial UK lobbyist was Commander Christopher Powell whose firm Watney and Powell (later Charles Barker, Watney and Powell) was established just before the Second World War. He was essentially a parliamentary draughtsman and an expert at guiding private bills through the House of Commons. The issue of professional lobbying was attracting the attention of MPs as far back as 1969. The growth of professional lobbying was a subsidiary theme of the Reports of the Select Committees on Members' Interests (Declaration) of both 1969 and 1974.

It is evident that lobbying by consultants grew considerably in the 1980s. One explanation is that the Thatcher government's distaste for vested interests meant that links with the civil service became more fragmented. Sponsorship divisions within government departments charged with looking after particular industries lost importance as a means of contact. Increased attention was paid to Parliament which was where contract lobbyists could be particularly helpful. When, in the 1983–84 session, a parliamentary committee examined the growth of the industry, a witness estimated that the political consultancy business had an annual fee income of £3.25 million. However, it was not until the 1980s that the scene changed and lobbying firms of the kind that we would recognise today were first established. Their turnover grew to an estimated £9 million by 1987, at which time it was

Table 2.1 Leading political consultants, December 2016–February 2017

Name of firm	Number of public affairs staff	Examples of clients
Newington Communications (formerly Bellenden)	46	Barratt, British Land, Church Commissioners
Weber Shandwick	45	Asda, Barclays, Volvo
Apco Worldwide	41	Mars, Microsoft, Reckitt Benckiser
Hanover Communications	41	GSK, Goldman Sachs, John Lewis
GK Strategy	33	Babcock, Leeds University, Travis Perkins
Remarkable	33	Anglian Water, Bovis Homes, National Grid
Edelman	31	Crossrail, Gatwick Airport, Sainsburys
Grayling	28	Lloyds Bank, National Grid, Virgin Trains
H + K Strategies	27	Shell, Tata Steel, Total
Burson-Marsteller	25	Aldi, Addison Lee, British Sugar

Source: Derived from Public Relations Consultants Association register

calculated that the industry was expanding by between 20 and 25 per cent each year.

Table 2.1 provides information about the ten leading commercial lobbyists in Britain in 2016/17, ranked in terms of numbers of staff engaged in public affairs activities. Although most of the clients are big corporations, they also serve public-sector clients such as local authorities and the National Health Service, charities and trade associations. Although all commercial lobbyists serve a wide range of clients, some evidently have areas of specialism; for example, H + K Strategies has a lot of clients in the area of energy supply. Outside the top ten, Curtin & Co. (17 staff) has an apparent specialism in the area of land, property and housing; Westbourne (17 staff) attracts many rail clients; and Westminster Advisory (22 staff) has a speciality in the area of health and social care. Some large firms make use of more than one contractor at the same time; for example, Centrica was using three during the period analysed.

What services do the leading commercial lobbyists offer? In their online presentations they talk about such matters as understanding the regulatory environment, getting a client's message across and building relationships with relevant decision-makers. For example, one of Newington Communications clients was Barratt Homes. Legislation on the National Planning Policy Framework (NPPF) required local councils to develop new local plans in order to meet local housing need. Newington's first task was to identify who the key decision-makers were. 'Newington initially assessed over thirty local authorities which were in the process of adopting new local plans, identifying the key stakeholders who would heavily influence where development would take place.' A targeted engagement strategy was developed, and 'Barratt was able to use our intelligence-led approach to build strategic relationships with high-level stakeholders, setting the groundwork for future discussions. In addition, face to face meetings also helped inform discussions with prospective regional stakeholders, to help generate political buy-in for future developments by Barratt' (Newington Communications, 2017: 1).

Weber Shandwick is part of a global company that has worked in particular with the nuclear industry in the past, but has a number of top-drawer clients. It advises prospective clients that

> Politics, policy and regulation have the power to knock you
> off course or to open up new opportunities. To prepare
> for and take advantage of policy changes, you have to

understand them. But politics can often seem difficult to analyse or predict. Weber Shandwick's public affairs team are experts in the political process. We can help you to understand what matters for your business – and help you to respond accordingly. Our consultants live for politics, whether that is played out in Parliament, a city hall, a town hall or a community hall. (Weber Shandwick, 2017)

APCO is another global lobbying firm. It has a diverse set of clients, but has particular expertise in food, consumer products and retail, where reputational issues can be important. It has worked with the food company Mars since 2005. 'Childhood obesity and obesity-related health problems are on the rise globally, with food companies facing increasing criticism and threats of adverse legislation' (APCO, 2017). The objective of the campaign for Mars was to turn critique into competitive advantage by developing a health and well-being ambition for a company that was perceived simply as a confectionery producer. In terms of issues management, APCO says that it can '[m]inimize the impact of issues before they become crises through: ally development; coalition building; crisis planning; Predictive Risk and Opportunity modelling (risk analysis); scenario planning; stakeholder mapping and engagement', among other services.

Hanover Communications is an independent agency that places particular emphasis on party conferences as a means of understanding policy trends and delivering a client's messages. 'Hanover builds bespoke contact programmes, organises convivial meals with the right mix of politicians, activists, advisors and, if appropriate, journalists; organises and promotes fringe events, and arranges exhibition conference stands and marketing material to promote your message or cause' (Hanover Communications, 2017).

GK Strategy offers research-led mechanisms for navigating highly regulated markets. Its largest specialism is healthcare, but it also has expertise in education, with a number of universities as clients. 'Informing and influencing the policy-making process is our core competency. We know how to expand political reach and utilise the full range of advocacy and parliamentary tools to realise our clients' objectives' (GK Strategy, 2017). What it offers to do is to audit a client's current relationships and then advise who they should develop relationships with to achieve policy objectives. It will then help to build these relationships, identifying opportunities to meet up with targets. For all the sophistication of this approach, the underlying message is that it is a question of who you need to know as much as what you want to tell them.

Remarkable Group claims to have a particular expertise in the area of planning permissions and development schemes, from local development to national infrastructure projects. It considers that very often this activity needs to be supported by a complementary, strategic government relations and public affairs plan. It is important to avoid charges of self-interested representation, and it sees its cutting edge in terms of communications strategies developed in 'an indirect way; thereby ensuring grassroots campaigns, engagement with think tanks & academics, the media and recognised commentators in particular sectors' (Remarkable Group, 2017).

Edelman, an American company, is the world's largest independent, global, public affairs and lobbying firm. It has some very distinguished clients. For over six decades it has taken pride in its achievements in building and positioning some of the biggest corporate and product brands in the world. 'Edelman pioneered the concept of public engagement – the intersection of public affairs and public relations that shifts perceptions and changes behaviour.' It believes in the importance of long-term stakeholder engagement based on trust. It shows a particular awareness of the way in which economic and political trends are shifting the way in which influence can be exerted.

> A significant transformation of power is in progress that affects policy decision-making. From a communications perspective, this means that the hierarchies of old are being replaced by more trusted peer-to-peer, horizontal networks. A new public opinion animated by citizens and consumers through real-time communication is disrupt-

ing intermediation and the traditional levers of power. (Edelman, 2017)

Grayling has teams in Holyrood and Cardiff as well as in Westminster. It has particular expertise in gaining support for infrastructure projects. The company has seen falling revenues in recent years, with UK revenue falling by a fifth in 2016. It has been going through a process of restructuring, with a number of new appointments. If nothing else, this is a reminder that political consultancy is a competitive market.

Hill and Knowlton, now known as H + K Strategies, was the first of the big American public relations firms to move into Europe in the mid-1950s. One past success was defeating a proposal for a tax on pesticides, mobilising opposition among farmers. It seeks to combine global reach with local knowledge. It claims that 'Our bipartisan team of lobbyists / strategists come out of the highest levels of government and thrive at the intersection of policy and politics. Trusted by both policymakers and clients, the team has deep connections with decision makers and regulators all over the world' (Hill and Knowlton, 2017).

Burson-Marsteller, founded in 1953, is one of the world's biggest public relations agencies. Its public affairs practice was started in 1974 and it was the first firm to develop a healthcare speciality in 1979. This has since become a major area of activity for many firms, given the importance of government spending to the healthcare industry. 'Our experienced team of public affairs consultants offer clients in-depth knowledge, understanding and insight into the political, parliamentary and regulatory landscape of the UK. We deliver public affairs programmes for clients that ensure their message is heard by the right people in the right places' (Burson-Marsteller, 2017).

The uncertainty created by Brexit is likely to increase the demand for the services of political consultants, both in London and in Brussels. Indeed, a number of firms have set up special Brexit units or are pitching their ability to help firms cope. Liedong and Rajwani (2017) suggest that 'In the battle for influence, there is a high likelihood that small firms will be squeezed out of the post-Brexit process due to the high costs involved and the limited voice they will have in Westminster. There might be instances of corporate dystopia where large and resource-endowed firms unfairly dominate the political agenda.'

Political consultants are active in providing the secretariats for all-party parliamentary groups, of which there are over 500 in Westminster. For example, Policy Connect provides the secretariat for eight all-party groups. The All-Party Parliamentary Water Group has been running for ten years and is described as providing 'a forum for Parliamentarians and interested stakeholders to monitor government and regulatory policy and maintain a dialogue with government, Parliament, the water sector and a wide range of other interested groups' (Connect, 2017).

The parliamentary groups have attracted criticism because of the large amounts spent on reports that often support the views of industry and that grant access to Parliament for companies and lobbyists. British Telecom backs the parliamentary internet, communications and technology forum known as Picfor, which gets access to more than 60 peers and MPs, providing a way for corporate representatives to meet with decision-makers. The drinks group Diageo has spent £11,200 on a beer group whose purposes include promoting 'the wholesomeness and enjoyment of beer and the unique role of the pub in society'. In 2017 it was announced that Alison White, who compiles the official register of lobbyists, was looking at all-party parliamentary groups to see if some should be added to her lists.

What is evident is that the biggest businesses are able to purchase the best advice on strategies and tactics, and are able to secure the access that allows them to exert influence on decision-makers. One area of concern is the movement of former civil servants into companies. 'One department that has seen more movement through the revolving door than any other is the Ministry of Defence. Since 1996, officials and military officers have taken up more than 3,500 jobs in arms and defence related companies' (Cave and Rowell, 2015: 70).

Concerns have also been expressed about a number of ministers and advisers taking on energy-sector jobs, including three former ministers from the Coalition government. In September 2017 the mid-sized energy supplier Ovo Energy hired Georgia Berry to be chief of staff to its chief executive. Until the 2017 general election she had been Theresa May's energy adviser and was one of the proponents of the price cap pledge that many energy companies opposed.

The Advisory Committee on Business Appointments (Acoba) has to consider and provide advice on offers of appointment to ministers or senior civil servants, whether paid or unpaid, that occur within two years of their leaving office. It has been criticised for a lack of rigour in its scrutiny, for example being too ready to accept the argument that the official being reviewed had nothing to do with the policy affecting his or her new employer. There has also been a long-term practice of secondments from private companies to government on the grounds that this improves mutual understanding, but there is concern that this may give companies opportunities to exert influence or at least improve their understanding of how a particular branch of government works.

3

How they lobby

OVER time the nature of lobbying in the UK has changed. At one time there were a number of tightly knit 'policy communities' made up of the executive branch of government (ministers and civil servants) and a small number of recognised lobbying organisations. A classic example was agriculture, where the NFU was given special status by the 1947 Agriculture Act. The subsidies paid to farmers were negotiated in a process known as the Annual Price Review. The Ministry of Agriculture, Fisheries and Food (MAFF) in effect acted as a spokesperson for farming interests within government. Policy communities didn't just confine the policy discussion to a limited range of actors; they also restricted the items that were the subject of discussion. For example, Toke and Marsh (2003) show that in the controversy over the introduction of genetically modified (GM) crops in Britain, the policy problem was largely defined in economic rather than environmental terms, reflecting the influence of the industry policy network. In so far as there was an environmental dimension, it was framed in terms of wildlife protection rather than wider concerns about possible impacts on human and animal health. Radical environmentalists, on the other hand, saw it as a clash between 'locally controlled organic farming and industrial farming controlled by multinational corporate interests' (Toke and Marsh, 2003: 234).

Lobbying has become both more fluid and more complex. Coalition and minority governments provide a range of lobbying targets, and assessing the balance of forces within government becomes more difficult. British membership of the EU meant that an increasing number of decisions were taken by Community institutions rather than by the UK government. Even when Britain leaves the EU, decisions taken there will still have implications for the UK. Parliament has become more assertive, with backbench MPs more willing to rebel. Even with majority governments, decisions have had to be modified in response to parliamentary pressure, including from the House of Lords. Select committees have become more effective interrogators of government policy. The devolved governments of Scotland, Wales and Northern Ireland have acquired increasing powers and decisions taken by them may influence the policy agenda in Westminster. The growth of social media has opened up a range of new possibilities for lobbying activities.

Policy communities have dissolved. In the case of agriculture, most of the decision-making was transferred to the EU, although the devolved administrations also secured a share. MAFF was abolished and replaced by Defra, which had a much wider remit. Environment, conservation and animal welfare organisations became part of the policy-making process, introducing new concerns and themes.

The policy agenda and the framing of issues

Anyone wanting to move policy in a new direction has to get their concerns placed on the policy agenda. That agenda is very crowded. The time of ministers and civil servants is constrained. Even if a department takes up an issue, it then has to fight for legislative time with other departments. This means that an issue needs sustained attention over a period of time. Social media campaigns may draw attention to an issue or attract public support, but they may not enable an issue to be pursued for the time required to secure change. In the meantime, well-resourced business lobbies may be able to challenge and water down the proposed policy initiative. The state is not simply a neutral arbiter of the validity of alternative evidence claims. In relation to the public debate on alcohol policy, 'Many of the objector arguments are out of kilter with government policy and are therefore never propagated in official discourse. State power is exercised diffusely in relation to the dissemination of knowledge and the omission of politically inconvenient research evidence from official literature reviews' (Hadfield, 2006: 210).

It is an important task of lobbies to influence how an issue is framed or defined and to challenge existing framings. The environmental lobby has been able largely to prevent the commercial cultivation of GM crops in Europe. They were able to portray these crops as a threat to the environment and potentially to human and animal health. In this task they were assisted by the fact that the projected introduction of GM crops came in the wake of a number of food scandals, most notably that of BSE, which led to several deaths among young people who had consumed offal-based meat products. The opponents of GM crops were able to present them as products that were being developed by American multinational companies whose primary motivation was profit. They were able to utilise language that portrayed them as a threat to everything that was 'natural', as 'Frankenstein foods'.

Framings are not necessarily evidence-based and may have no relation to the underlying science. It is the image that is conveyed that is important. Consider the example of the 'rogue badger', a creature that does not exist, but that came to exert an influence on policy. At one time officials had a benevolent view of the badger, which was seen as a means of controlling insects and other pests. It was thought that bovine TB, which afflicts cattle, had been eradicated, but when it reappeared, farmers' organisations and veterinarians drew attention to what they saw as a reservoir of the disease in badgers. The invention of the concept of the rogue badger involved an admission that badgers could be harmful, but this was confined to a subgroup of 'deviant' badgers. These might be eradicated by expert marksmen, although it was never clear how one might distinguish a rogue badger from the badger population in general.

The policy on bovine TB has seen a series of reports and

policy reviews. At one time badger setts were gassed, but then this policy was suspended, and currently the culling of badgers by shooting occurs in designated areas where there are high levels of bovine TB. However, no agreement has ever been reached on the framing of the policy. The balance of influence between the different lobbies has swayed backwards and forwards, depending in part on the government in office. As far as wildlife organisations are concerned, the badger is being targeted when it should be treated as a valued, innocent animal. They argue that the role of cattle-to-cattle transmission has been underplayed and that there is no scientific evidence regarding the mode of transmission from badgers to cattle. Farmers and vets insist that badgers are a significant source of the disease and that culling is therefore necessary. The emotive nature of the debate, with both sides taking entrenched positions, has meant that other policy options such as encouraging farms to take biosecurity measures, for example fencing badger latrines or making entry to cattle sheds more difficult, have been underplayed. Strong opposed lobbies can lead to an absence of agreement on how policy should be framed and underperformance or paralysis in policy.

Obesity attracted considerable media attention in 2004. The present phase of interest in the subject was largely started by investigations conducted by the World Health Organization. However, reports by an international organisation would not attract such extensive interest unless they pushed a number of political buttons. Obesity is on the increase in Western societies and it is a visible problem that can be easily documented and dramatised by the media. The broader significance of the issue lies in its links with health policy and the increased risks of illness and mortality linked with obesity. Such a link attracts the interest of government because it wishes to promote a healthier population, not least because of the ever-increasing costs of public healthcare.

High levels of salt in processed food form part of this debate, and this is an issue that has attracted particular attention in Britain. Essentially, manufacturers use salt in processed food products such as bread to make them more palatable to consumers. It is very difficult even for well-informed consumers to avoid products containing high levels of salt. Research suggests a clear link between salt levels in food and high blood pressure, increasing the risk of heart disease and stroke. The food industry has tried to answer these criticisms by claiming that there is no such thing as an unhealthy food, only an unhealthy diet. It has been suggested that the food industry is where the tobacco industry was about forty years ago, when the link between cigarette smoking and cancer was firmly established. The parallel is not an exact one, because people can survive without tobacco, but they are unlikely to be able to manage without processed food. However, it is interesting that one response of the food industry has been to introduce 'light', that is, low-salt, versions of its top brands. Light cigarettes have now been discredited, and the food industry could find itself faced with similar legal difficulties to the tobacco industry if it makes claims that are unsustainable.

The food industry has shown signs of losing the debate over salt levels in particular, despite a public relations campaign by the Salt Manufacturers' Association and other parts of the industry to persuade health professionals and the general population that the evidence in relation to salt is not clear and that no action is justified. One of the reasons for the industry's lack of success in presenting its case has been the knowledge-based campaigning of organisations such as Consensus Action on Salt and Health (CASH). CASH was set up in 1996 in response to the refusal by the Chief Medical Officer to endorse the recommendations of an official advisory committee that people should reduce their salt intake. It was chaired by a consultant in cardiovascular medicine at St George's Hospital in London, and based its arguments on scientific and medical evidence. CASH aims to counter the claims made by the industry by drawing on the wealth of scientific evidence that links high salt intake to health problems. CASH has set itself the realistic objective of reaching a consensus with food manufacturers and suppliers that salt does have adverse health effects, and persuading them to gradually reduce the levels of salt in processed foods.

There is a very strong producers' lobby on these issues, with the NFU, the British Retail Consortium, the British Hospitality Association and the Food and Drink Federation taking a leading role. The issue is also a difficult one for government to handle and it has been possible for the industry to use the classic tactic of exploiting divisions within government. A number of policy options were explored within government, but their selection was influenced by New Labour's preference for a good working relationship with business, which led it to choose voluntary regulation wherever possible. This was reinforced by concerns that the government could be accused of creating a 'nanny state' if it intervened too much in what people eat. The coalition of opponents widened when ITV complained that a ban would damage its ability to produce original programmes for children because of the potential diminution of advertising revenues.

The clear divisions on this issue between different government departments offered openings for industry lobbyists. In June 2004 the public health minister, Melanie Johnson, leaked a document that 'named and shamed' 27 food companies for refusing to make substantial cuts in the salt content of their food. The Department of Health's view was that it was necessary to keep up pressure on the industry in order to achieve a satisfactory voluntary agreement. However, other government departments thought that the Health Department's approach had damaged the delicate and long-term process of persuading the food industry to change its behaviour. The food industry argued that the episode had damaged confidence in the process, although it chose to characterise it as bungled news handling rather than an aggressive act by government. The fact that departments were briefing against each other exposed the divisions in government and allowed the food industry to seize the initiative and present itself as an advocate of constructive dialogue which had been mistreated.

Health and consumer groups have been successful in attracting media attention to the issue, placing it on the political agenda and counteracting arguments that there is no problem. Faced by a well-resourced producer lobby, they have been far less successful in winning support for the policy solutions they favour, and outcomes in terms of the salt intake that arises from processed food have so far changed less than medical experts would like. However, in 2014 targets were announced for salt reduction in 76 specific food groups that contribute most to people's salt intakes, which are to be achieved by December 2017.

The framing of issues is a highly contested process. Issues need to be placed on the policy agenda, but also kept there. Reliable evidence can help to structure a debate, particularly in relation to health issues, but sometimes the evidence is contested and more emotive framings may prevail, as in the case of badgers and bovine TB. However, it is important to remember that the political process is not just about evidence, which can appear a rather technocratic approach, but also about the values we attach to processes and outcomes.

Government consultations

The Blair government initiated a new policy of formal written consultations on policy developments, starting with a code of practice on written consultation in 2000. The stated intention was to make written consultations more effective, opening decision-making to as wide a range of people as possible. The system is still in place, with consultations, which normally take the form of a series of questions, being opened practically every day. Indeed, consultations are sometimes released in batches, which strains the resources of those responding to them. The latest set of consultation principles issued in 2016 requires civil servants to consider the full range of those affected by a policy and whether representative groups exist. If necessary, specific groups should be targeted, ensuring that they are aware of the consultation and how they can access it.

Does this system ensure that a wider range of views are taken into account in policy-making? Once again one comes up against the reality that businesses are better resourced to respond to specific and often highly technical policy issues. 'Within the existing consultation processes, large ... firms and representative bodies are generally well prepared to respond to consultations, and have the resources to do so' (Rutter et al., 2017: 22). For example, Marks and Spencer often adds its support to responses from one of its main trade associations, such as the CBI or the British Retail Consortium. However, it also makes its own individual responses, 17 in all between 2011 and 2016. These responses covered subjects ranging from the Northern Ireland carrier bag charge to consultation on the fifth carbon budget.

A recurrent concern is that consultations start too late in the policy process and are focused on technical details and challenges of implementation, rather than the rationale for changes or different ways in which a policy objective might be achieved. To put it another way, the existing framing of the policy is taken as a given, and the focus is on how the policy might be put into effect. If the scope of a policy is narrowly defined, it may fail to achieve desired outcomes.

The responses received to a consultation are likely to be viewed through the prism of existing policy, particularly by the civil servant responsible for writing a report summarising the responses. One such civil servant commented, 'You give weight to things that are related to political priorities ... Then you give extra weighting to some organizations rather than others – the Local Government Association is a big organization and what they say is usually worth reporting' (quoted in Page and Jenkins, 2005: 129). 'The resources that responding to consultation requires also means there is much less input from those who are not as well organized, and who are not primed to respond to multiple government consultations' (Rutter et al., 2017: 22). The needs of bigger businesses may be taken care of, but the challenges faced by micro businesses may receive much less attention. The consultation process set out in the Corporation Tax Road Map could be interpreted as giving more weight to business interests. For example, the Corporate Tax Reform Liaison Committee that led the process was composed of one

MP and representatives from large corporations; there was no representation of trade unions or of civil society.

The Scottish government has made a conscious effort to ensure that consultation processes are not limited to the 'usual suspects'. Some traditional interests were slow to develop relationships with the Scottish government and parliament, while voluntary groups took advantage of the new opportunities. In general, groups feel engaged and listened to, assisted by the proximity of decision-makers, and are positive about the experience of devolution. 'However, the extent to which the Scottish process differs from the UK is debatable' (Cairney and McGarvey, 2013: 169).

Does the formal consultation process open policy-making to a variety of voices and perspectives? Or is it a means of legitimising policy, so that government can say that it has consulted widely before putting a policy into effect? It would seem to be more of the latter, with considerable weight given to existing interests. In many ways it is a highly managed process, with organisations responding to questions set by government.

Action through the courts

Since the 1980s increasing use has been made of judicial reviews of government decisions. If one excludes the large number of appeals relating to immigration and asylum, the number of judicial reviews has levelled out at about 2,000 a year since the mid-1990s. What happens in a judicial review is that a judge reviews the lawfulness of a decision made by a public body. In other words, the focus is on the way in which a decision has been made, rather than the rights and wrongs of the conclusion reached. The court does not substitute what it thinks is the 'correct' decision. The public body may be able to make the same decision again, providing that it does so in a lawful way. In general, there are three grounds for bringing judicial review proceedings:

- Illegality – the decision was not taken in accordance with the relevant body or law or went beyond the powers of the decision-making body.
- Irrationality – it was not taken reasonably or no reasonable person could have taken it.
- Procedural irregularity, such as a failure to consult properly or to act in accordance with natural justice or the related procedural rules.

NGOs saw judicial review as a means to challenge government decisions, particularly in relation to environmental and planning issues. Government became increasingly concerned at the way in which these reviews were delaying decisions, even if they did not succeed in overturning them. The Coalition government therefore proposed a number of measures to limit access to judicial review. However, these proposals were highly controversial and were considerably watered down in the legislative process, eventually leading to the Criminal Justice and Courts Act 2015.

In disputes over licensing laws, leisure corporations are able to overcome community activists in courtroom battles. 'As in other spheres of regulatory practice, such as planning law, a whole legal and extra-legal industry ... developed to assist applicants in their navigation of rough regulatory waters' (Hadfield, 2006: 173). Use was made of law firms, consultancy companies, individual experts, trade associations but, above all, a small and elite band of specialist licensing barristers. Government stood aside from the debate on alcohol-related harm, placing its faith in the individual responsibility of the consumer and supplier of alcohol, health education campaigns and self-regulation by the industry. These measures clearly did not deal with problems such as binge drinking. Clear inequalities existed in court between the licensing trade teams and their opponents.

Social media

'Social media are Internet-based platforms that allow the creation and exchange of user-generated content' (Margetts et al., 2016: 5). They include such platforms as Facebook, Twitter, YouTube and Instagram, but new platforms are appearing all the time. The question that their development raises in relation to lobbying is how transformative are they? Do they offer new means of citizen involvement and engagement that overcome some of the inbuilt inequalities in the existing system of lobbying?

What they clearly do is reduce the resource costs involved in setting up and publicising a campaign to close to zero. This undermines one of the key advantages enjoyed by established lobby groups such as those representing business. Conventional forms of organisation become less important as intermediaries between citizens and government. However, one must be careful of pushing this 'organising without organisations' approach too far. Social media have facilitated the emergence of entirely new kinds of lobbying organisations. They also make it much easier to mobilise support for a campaign. Indeed, one of their important roles may be to make individuals aware that the views they hold are not as unorthodox as they thought, but are shared by many others.

However, they do not unclutter the public space; indeed they make it more cluttered. There are even more agenda items competing for attention. We are aware of the campaigns that gain momentum, but not of the far greater number that fail. In part they fail because they do not resonate with concerns that are widely shared, but it may also be a question of how they are presented. The possession of relevant skills still matters, even if they are different from the skills deployed in conventional lobbying.

Inspired by advocacy groups such as MoveOn in the United States, 38 Degrees was formed in 2009. It refers to the angle at which snowflakes form an unstoppable avalanche. Members are able to suggest campaigns and they are polled on which one should be pursued. It claims to have three million members, although an individual counts as a member once he or she has signed a petition or undertaken any other action from their website, blog, Facebook page or Twitter handle. It claims to have stopped the UK government's plan to privatise forests and to have blocked a mega-dairy in Lincolnshire, although others were involved in those campaigns. It should also be noted that the claims relate to stopping policy proposals rather than getting new ones adopted.

38 Degrees also exists less in a pure social media space than might be apparent. It relies on mainstream media to demonstrate to its members that its campaigns are making an impact and moving towards a successful outcome. When 'professional media attention fades, interdependence turns to dependence, and a 38 degrees campaign is more likely to falter' (Chadwick and Dennis, 2017: 43). Digital network repertoires coexist with gaining professional news media coverage.

Transaction costs are undoubtedly low for an individual clicking online to support a campaign, but can what is sometimes called 'slacktivism' generate a sustained campaign that brings about policy change? It can be difficult to sustain 'mobilizations that lack institutions or organization' (Margetts et al., 2016: 218). Followers can become disillusioned by the lack of policy response.

In 2016 a woman in a temporary position was sent home without pay for failing to wear high heels at work. The case attracted considerable interest and 152,400 people signed a petition on the issue. The complainant subsequently gave evidence before the Petitions and Women and Equalities Committees of the House of Commons. However, the government ruled out a change in the law because it said that the existing legislation was adequate. Rather more successful was a website set up by a group of teaching unions called schoolcuts.org.uk, which allowed parents to type in a postcode and see exactly how much money their school was going to lose as a result of reductions in funding. Using data obtained under the Freedom of Information Act 2000, the public was given information about how badly government policy might affect their children. Announcing extra funding for schools, the education secretary, Justine Greening, complained in her Commons statement about the website 'worrying parents' with 'out-of-date data' (Hansard, 2017: cols 569–70).

Some writers take the view that the equilibrium of power will be different in the twenty-first century because of the existence of an online world. 'The Internet will remain a force for redistribution of power because of the ease with which it assists mobilization, given that it can ensure that groups with the most resources do not always win' (Margetts et al., 2016: 216). Of course, the best-resourced groups did not always win before the advent of the Internet. It can certainly place issues on the political agenda; whether it can then overcome resistance to policy change on the part of established groups is a more open question.

Advocacy coalitions

One way for campaigning organisations facing entrenched business lobbies to enhance their influence is to form advocacy coalitions. Such an approach can increase the resources that are available by pooling them. It can also give access to different skill sets, for example constructing an evidence-based case or appealing to the public through a media campaign. Different organisations may have access to particular professional groups or segments of the public which they can mobilise to boost the campaign.

Of course, there are downsides as well. Organisations want to maintain their distinctive identities so that they can continue to appeal to their memberships. They may not agree on policy objectives or how they should be achieved, and this could lead to a watering down of the message and a 'lowest common denominator' approach, which would then limit meaningful policy change. However, these challenges can be overcome.

The Alcohol Health Alliance (AHA), which was launched in 2007, brings together over forty organisations. They have a shared interest in reducing the damage caused to health by alcohol misuse. The AHA has a strong core anchor in the Royal College of Physicians (RCP), giving access to its resources and network of contacts. Membership was initially restricted to a tightly knit group, although this has expanded over time. 'Care was taken from the start that, as far as possible, members would share core policy beliefs' (Thom et al., 2016: 310). There has been general agreement about the policies that need to be implemented, although there has been disagreement about specific issues such as whether there should be a ban on alcohol advertising.

One challenge that the AHA faced was the framing of the issue. The UK government and the alcohol industry preferred to focus on the minority of problem drinkers. This led to a criminal-justice-led approach to policy, focusing on binge drinking and problems associated with the night-time economy, which tended to put the Home Office in the driving seat rather than the Department of Health. It should be noted that the government derives substantial tax revenues from alcohol, giving the Treasury an interest in the issue. The AHA was concerned with issues of population-wide drinking. This led to a need to convince the public as well as decision-makers, given that the public might view restrictions on consumption as a threat to an enjoyable activity which they believed they indulged in in moderation.

'The AHA successfully positioned the group as an influential stakeholder within the policy sphere and had considerable impact in re-framing the discourse around alcohol' (Thom et al., 2016: 20). They made issues of price part of the debate about alcohol, pointing out that alcohol is 60 per cent more affordable now than it was in 1980. Their emphasis on minimum unit pricing (MUP), which sets a floor price below which a unit of alcohol may not be sold, could have detracted from other policy options. However, they were able to use the tactic of getting it on to the policy agenda by securing its adoption in Scotland. Minimum unit pricing was passed by the Scottish Parliament in May 2012, but implementation was delayed due to a legal challenge from the alcohol industry. Over the course of the legal process, the Scottish courts twice ruled that MUP is legal, and the alcohol industry then made one final appeal to the UK's Supreme Court. This appeal, heard in November 2017, was unsuccessful, and minimum unit pricing for alcohol can now be implemented in Scotland.

It is also possible for campaigning organisations to take advantage of the fact that business is not a homogeneous interest, and to form alliances with more progressive segments of the business community. These differences are particularly marked in the case of climate change. For some firms, particularly in fossil fuels, tackling climate change can be seen to represent a major threat to their business. For other firms, for example those operating in renewables, mitigating climate change represents a business opportunity. At one end of the spectrum are firms and sectors that produce fossil fuels or are highly dependent on them. They are likely to attract political support from energy-intensive industries that are sensitive to input prices, such as steel, glass, aluminium, paper and ceramics. At the other end of the spectrum are those firms that are actively involved in the green economy and are engaged in the development and application of new technologies.

As far as companies that have an incentive to take action on climate change are concerned, insurance and reinsurance companies face the prospect of enormous liabilities from rising weather-related claims. The Association of British Insurers claims that an increase in the frequency or severity of extreme weather events could mean that insurers would have to increase premiums to stay viable. The insurance industry therefore believes that it faces some real threats from climate change in terms of increased uncertainty, particularly in relation to pricing its products. It considers that if it responds to those challenges in the right way, it can turn a threat into a market opportunity that would also enhance the industry's reputation. The industry wants to be seen as part of the solution rather than as a barrier to progress. Unlike, say, the coal industry, climate change will not reduce the total volume of insurance business, but there is a greater risk of making unpredictable losses, so anything that can be done to reduce that risk is beneficial.

Influencing the European Union

As more decisions were taken by the EU, it became an important venue for lobbying activity. It is difficult to estimate precisely the number of lobbyists in Brussels, but it is thought that there are at least 25,000. The voluntary EU transparency register listed over 11,307 organisations in June 2017, although it is generally accepted that this list is incomplete. Of these, 5,595 were in-house lobbyists and trade, business and professional associations. Professional consultancies are very active in Brussels. According to lobbyfacts.eu there were ten firms spending over €2.5m a year on lobbying in November 2016, based on data derived from the EU transparency register. Of these, the largest was Fleishman-Hillard, which spent €6.25m, but some of the names were familiar from the UK: Burson-Marseller (€5m), Hill and Knowlton (€3.75m) and Grayling (€2.5m).

At one time, lobbying activity was concentrated on the directorates-general (the equivalent of ministries) of the European Commission. This was supplemented by contacts with national governments, although as the number of member states increased, it became more difficult for any one member state to influence policy outcomes. With the arrival of co-legislation, the European Parliament became a much more important venue for lobbyists.

Effective lobbying requires a permanent presence in Brussels and this is expensive, given the need for office accommodation and a minimum number of personnel. Business lobbyists have predominated in Brussels. BusinessEurope represents business as a whole, being made up of individual company members and national federations such as the CBI. In 2016 it spent over €4m on lobbying and had 30 declared lobbyists. It had 168 meetings with the European Commission during the year. The European Round Table brings together around fifty chief executives and chairmen of major multinational companies such as BP, Philips, Vodafone and Royal Dutch Shell. It is selective in the issues it tackles, focusing on those it sees as being of major importance.

There are also less prominent but still influential

organisations. AMISA2 was originally set up in 1994 and holds monthly breakfast meetings with a senior speaker from the EU institutions. There have been 293 such meetings since 1994, generally with senior-level officials such as cabinet members, director generals or their deputies. It claims that it is not a lobbying organisation, but 'corporations get plenty of opportunity to ask questions about issues which concern their business'. Member companies pay €4,000 a year and include Airbus, BASF, ExxonMobil, Google and Total. 'These corporations represent some of Brussels' biggest lobbyists declaring at least €28,589,000 lobby spend for the last year for which figures are available, and holding 73 European Parliament access passes' (Corporate Europe Observatory, 2016a: 4).

At an industry level, business associations are organised as federations of member-state associations, although some industries, such as volume car production, have direct membership associations and others have a combination of firm and association members. Some of these sector associations are bigger than BusinessEurope. For example, the influential European Chemical Industries Council (CEFIC) spent €12.1m on lobbying in 2016, had 48 accredited lobbyists, and held 53 meetings with the European Commission, effectively one a week. Big companies have their own government relations divisions in Brussels and they also make use of political consultants. Some national organisations such as the CBI and NFU have their own offices in Brussels.

In 2017 Google was fined €2.4 billion by EU competition regulators for illegally favouring its own shopping service. The company was expected to appeal. It spent €4.25m on lobbying in Brussels in 2015, according to the EU transparency register, and had 14 staff members directly involved in lobbying the EU. There was also likely to have been extensive lobbying of member-state governments. Google was a member of AMISA2, BusinessEurope and DigitalEurope, the trade association for the digital technology industry. When it first joined the lobby register, its annual spend on lobbying was €600,000–€700,000. Since then, its lobby spend has increased by 700 per cent:

Google is, without doubt, one of the most active lobbyists in Brussels. With 120 lobby meetings held since December 2014 with a commissioner, cabinet member or director-general (there have probably been many more meetings with lower level officials, not to mention MEPs, but these are not systematically published), Google is second only to Business Europe (140 meetings) in terms of lobby organisations with the best access to the elite of the Commission. (Cann, 2016: 1)

The European Parliament was seen as a venue that was more open to public interest lobbying, but that has changed as it has become a more significant player in the decision-making process. In-house groups, mostly associations and companies, account for more than 50 per cent of the accredited organisations and accredited persons (2,163 persons and 850 organisations). Professional consultancies account for 14 per cent of accredited organisations and 18 per cent of accredited organisations (735 persons and 211 organisations). NGOs account for 23 per cent of both categories (977 persons and 365 organisations) (Coen and Katsaitis, 2015). The EU does try to redress the balance by providing funding support for NGOs and it is estimated that around 40 per cent of them do receive some funding.

Brexit poses particular challenges for lobbying groups. Business does not generally see it as in its interests, while trade unions are concerned about the erosion of worker protection and NGOs fear that environmental protection will be weakened. Considerable resources therefore have to be devoted to seeking to influence the negotiation process to secure a least bad outcome. Given the complexity of the process, and the range of issues that have to be resolved, well-resourced groups are once again at an advantage:

In the battle for influence, there is a high likelihood that small firms will be squeezed out of the post-Brexit policy process due to the high costs involved and the limited voice they will have at Westminster. There might be cases of corporate dystopia where large and resource-endowed firms unfairly dominate the political agenda. (Liedong and Rajwani, 2017)

Lobbyists will still need to exert influence on the EU after Brexit, not least on behalf of British multinational companies with operations within the EU, although the way in which that is done will depend on the form that Brexit takes. The UK will still be affected by EU decisions, but as a rule and policy taker rather than as a rule and policy maker. The decisions that the EU takes will need to be monitored, even if the opportunities to influence them will be much more limited.

4

Lobbying in action

THIS chapter considers three case studies of lobbying in action: the campaign to reduce sugar consumption; issues relating to fixed odds betting terminals (FOBTs); and the future of the Green Belt. Two of these cases relate to potential harm: in the case of sugar, to the population in general; in the case of fixed odds betting terminals, to a subset of those who gamble. The issue of the Green Belt relates to deeply held values in one section of the population.

An underlying theme of this chapter is the way in which issues are 'framed'. This in turn relates to shifts over time in both public and expert opinion. For example, at one time smoking was even recommended by some doctors, for example as a means of calming 'nerves'. Non-smokers were often seen as odd or unsociable. Certainly, advocacy of non-smoking was a fringe activity. As more evidence became available regarding the harm caused by smoking, medical opinion shifted. Tobacco companies sought to defend smoking on libertarian grounds, but this became more difficult when evidence mounted about the harm caused by passive smoking, leading to more stringent restrictions.

As Rose (1974: 353) points out, 'The likelihood of any group gaining wide popular support for its demands depends upon the congruence between group demand and the values, beliefs and emotions widely diffused in the culture.' Rose (1974: 254–5) developed a sixfold typology of the congruence between a group's goals and wider cultural norms, which is presented here with updated examples:

1. *Harmony between pressure group goals and general cultural norms.* Organisations opposing cruelty to children and animals are obvious examples, yet each of them raises interesting questions about the stability and effectiveness of such relationships. The RSPCA attracted widespread press criticism for its abrasive style after its £330,000 prosecution of the Heythrop Hunt and for being too aggressive towards some pet owners, whose animals had been seized and euthanised. In June 2017 the charity was warned to bring its governance up to the standard the public would expect by the Charity Commission. Similarly, concern about child cruelty did not lead to effective action against sexual predators on children for many years.

2. *A gradual increase in the acceptability of political values supporting pressure group demands.* Homosexual acts between consenting males were made legal in 1967 and since then there has been a shift in public attitudes and the introduction of gay marriage (outside of Northern Ireland).

3. *Bargaining with fluctuating support from cultural norms.* An organisation such as the CPRE may draw on values of 'Englishness', but these may come into conflict with other priorities, as the case study on the Green Belt in this chapter shows.

4. *Advocacy in the face of cultural indifference.* Founded in 1929 as the Pedestrians' Association, Living Streets, as it is now called, has always been relatively weak compared to motoring organisations and, more recently, the cyclists' lobby. Its greatest success has been its 'Walk to School' campaign, which draws on values regarding safety for children.

5. *Advocacy in opposition to long-term cultural trends.* The advocates of restricted shop opening on Sundays (trade unions and religious bodies) found it impossible to stem the combined effect of commercial pressures from retailers and apparent consumer preferences.

6. *Conflict between cultural values and pressure group goals.* Campaigns by animal rights activists against angling, which is a popular recreational activity, have made little headway.

Moreover, many of the most effective campaigns to protect both marine and freshwater ecosystems have been launched or propelled by those who engage in fishing as a sport.

Campaigners need to be sensitive to changing cultural values and how they can shape their campaigns to resonate with them, without, of course, abandoning their principles. Lent (2012: 47) shows how 'the gay and lesbian movement of the 1990s espoused distinct values to that of the 1970s as a result of the changed social and political context within which it found itself operating'. Framing and tactics that worked in the 1970s would not have been appropriate in the different context of the 1990s.

Not so sweet: sugar

The effects of excessive sugar consumption have become a matter of serious concern for public health specialists. Sugar is not a necessary source of energy, which can be obtained from other carbohydrates.

> The incidence of obesity and type 2 diabetes, along with the sometimes serious consequences of those diseases, is rapidly increasing. There is a direct link between consumption of sugars and dental caries as well as a possible link between consuming excess sugars and high cholesterol, high blood pressure, some cancers and non-alcoholic liver disease. (Action on Sugar, 2017)

There has been particular concern about the relationship between sugar consumption and increasing child obesity.

The food industry has mobilised to oppose public policy initiatives on sugar consumption, such as mandatory sugar reductions, labelling and sugar taxes. The issue is of particular concern to the sugar industry, which uses both cane sugar and beet sugar as raw materials. In the EU it has the support of farmers who grow beet sugar. However, it is also of importance to the wider food and drink industry, which sees the addition of sugar as a way of making its products palatable and attractive to consumers.

The issue is one that is fought out both at the EU and the domestic level.

> [The] leverage which food industry giants have over EU decision-making has helped the sugar industry to see off many of these threats to its profit margins. Key trade associations, companies, and lobby groups relating to sugary food and drinks together spend an estimated €21.3 million annually to lobby the European Union. (Corporate European Observatory, 2016b: 3)

The principal lobby in the UK is the Food and Drink Federation (FDF), which represents brands including Mars, Nestlé, Cadbury and Kellogg's. The agri-food sector is a major component in the UK economy in terms of both value added and employment.

Action on Sugar was set up in 2014 by the team that had been campaigning on salt through Consensus Action on Salt and Health (CASH). It had a staff of three in 2017. It seeks to reach a consensus with the food industry and government over the harmful effects of a high-sugar diet, and to bring about a reduction in the amount of sugar in processed foods. Like CASH, Action on Sugar is setting targets for the food industry to progressively reduce the amount of sugar in its products, so that consumers do not notice the difference in taste. Diabetes UK and the British Heart Foundation are also active on the issue.

Both at a domestic and EU level, the food and drink industry has used a range of strategies. 'Unfortunately the European Commission and the European Food Safety Authority (EFSA) have been far too willing to listen to industry's messages, reflecting their all too often overly close relationship with the food and drink industry' (Corporate European Observatory, 2016b: 5). The strategies deployed have included challenging regulation through legal threats, sponsoring physical activity as an alternative to legislative action and sponsoring industry-friendly scientific research. Four of the five studies relied upon by EFSA when it ruled in 2010 that there was not enough scientific evidence to set upper limits for added sugars were industry-funded. 'Trade association FoodDrinkEurope spent approximately €1 billion in a successful campaign against a EU-wide "traffic light" food labelling scheme that is most recommended by health experts and consumer groups' (Corporate Europe Observatory, 2016b: 6).

The championing of weak voluntary schemes as a substitute for legislation and regulation is particularly relevant in the UK case. In 2016 the government launched a sugar reformulation programme as its response to childhood obesity. All sectors of the food and drinks industry were challenged to reduce overall sugar content across a range of products that contribute to children's sugar intake by at least 20 per cent by 2020. This could be achieved through a reduction of sugar levels in products, reducing portion size or shifting purchasing towards lower-sugar alternatives. Public Health England was put in charge of the programme, which applies to all sectors of industry – retailers, manufacturers and the out-of-home sector (e.g. restaurants, takeaways and cafés). The programme will initially focus on the nine categories that make the largest contributions to children's sugar intake: breakfast cereals, yoghurts, biscuits, cakes, confectionery, morning goods (e.g. pastries), puddings, ice cream and sweet spreads.

The FDF said that a 20 per cent cut 'won't be technically possible or acceptable to UK consumers'. It argued that instead of setting 'arbitrary targets', there should be a 'continuous journey'. Action on Sugar responded that the FDF had said exactly the same thing on salt reduction: '"We can't do it. There's no point." It wasn't hard and it was done' (Smyth, 2017: 2).

Campaigners were unimpressed by the government's response, released in the middle of August 2016, which they considered to fall well short of a comprehensive strategy. The House of Commons Health Committee commented that 'several key areas for action that could have made the strategy more effective were removed' (House of Commons Health Committee, 2017: 11). Theresa May ditched most of a childhood obesity strategy proposed by David Cameron and abandoned plans for tough curbs on two-for-one deals and the advertising of junk foods during family TV programmes. Table 4.1 summarises the differences between the recommendations made by the House of Commons Health Committee in its 2015 report on childhood obesity and the policy outcome in 2017, based on an analysis by David Buck of the King's Fund.

Theresa May was criticised for siding with the big business lobby instead of public health in one of her first major policy decisions. Action on Sugar said that it was a 'tragedy' that May had not done more on sugar. The industry emphasised the threat of job losses and slower growth against the background of the uncertainty created by Brexit. Some familiar arguments were used against effective action:

> First, they say it's bad for business. In fact, obviously any action by government is by definition 'bad for business'. Two, it is claimed that obesity isn't really caused by sugar or junk food, but something (anything) else — lack of investment in sport, too much television, you name it. Three (and this is fundamental) it's all just an excuse by government, which wants to get ever bigger, crush our liberties, and tell us how to live our lives. (Ashley, 2016)

Public health campaigners on sugar have made some headway, notably in terms of the sugar tax that was introduced in the 2016 budget. It is attractive to government as it is a source of additional revenue that could be expanded in future. The levy is due to come into force in April 2018 and places a tax of 18 pence per litre on soft drinks with more than 5 g of sugar per 100 ml; and a second, higher band of 24 pence on those with more than 8 g of sugar per 100 ml. It is expected that the tax will raise £520m in its first year of operation. Manufacturers have started to reformulate some of their products in anticipation of the tax; for example, in Lucozade and Ribena the sugar content has been cut by half. However, a test of its effectiveness will be whether it leads to price increases on drinks with high sugar content. Businesses may choose to spread the price increases across all their products, reducing the targeting effect. It is evident that the

Table 4.1   Differences between the Health Select Committee recommendations and the government's childhood obesity plan

Health Select Committee recommendations	Childhood obesity plan
Strong controls on price promotions of unhealthy food and drinks	No mention of price promotions
Tougher controls on marketing and advertising of unhealthy food and drink	No mention of marketing and advertising
A centrally led reformulation programme to reduce sugar in food and drink	Targets in nine categories of food contributing most to children's sugar intake, but action is voluntary until 2020 and no mention of penalties or sanctions
A sugary drinks tax on full-sugar soft drinks, with all proceeds targeted to help those children at greatest risk of obesity	[Sugar 'tax' to be introduced in April 2018]. Benefit of the doubt but the devil is in the detail – proceeds to go to school sports and unclear whether targeted at those at greatest risk
Labelling of single portions of products with added sugar to show sugar content as teaspoons	Labelling mentioned, in context of Brexit and greater flexibility, but no details or commitments
Improved education and information about diet	No mention of education or information about diet
Stronger powers for local authorities to tackle the environment leading to obesity	No mention of stronger powers for local authorities
Early intervention to offer help to families affected by obesity	'Recommitting' to Healthy Start Voucher Scheme; income from sugar level to schools including an incentive premium

Source: House of Commons Health Committee 2017: 8

industry has been able to fight an effective rearguard action to protect its position.

Fixed odds betting terminals (FOBTs)

FOBTs, sometimes called B2 machines following their classification in the 2005 Gambling Act, were introduced into betting shops in 1999, with a small number of high-margin games available. Changes to the taxation of gambling (the introduction of a gross tax on profits) came into effect in October 2001 and allowed the betting industry to introduce new, lower-margin products, such as roulette, to FOBTs. This led to a growth in the numbers of FOBTs in betting shops.

Up to four machines can be sited in a single betting premises. The maximum stake on a single bet is £100; the maximum prize is £500. They allow customers to bet up to £100 every 20 seconds on electronic casino games, with some punters racking up huge losses within hours. Campaigners against them describe them as the 'crack cocaine' of gambling, arguing that the quick-fire play and high stakes encourage customers to chase losses. The Association of British Bookmakers (ABB) claims that the average spend is between £5 and £6 nationally, with customers staying on a gaming machine for around ten minutes on average. According to the Gambling Commission, £1.7bn was spent on FOBTs between October 2014 and September 2015, accounting for 56 per cent of betting shops' profits. This figure has since increased to £1.8bn, and the amount spent on them was only just behind the amount contributed by online betting.

The Association of British Bookmakers is the trade association for Britain's high street betting shops and claims to represent 80 per cent of the sector. It had a staff of seven in 2017. The regulatory body for the industry, the Gambling Commission, states that it works closely with trade associations such as the ABB. The horse racing industry is also interested in any measures taken to restrict FOBTs which could lead to substantial closures of betting shops. Horse racing is partially funded by a tax on profits made from wagers on races. The advertising industry, particularly television, also benefits considerably from advertising placed by betting companies. They also engage extensively in shirt sponsorship for football clubs.

Those opposed to FOBTs have an unusual mixture of moral and commercial motivations. There is a difficult dilemma in terms of balancing the enjoyment of the majority who gamble without experiencing harm with the protection of a minority who are at risk. One of the issues that has arisen is just how much public concern there is about FOBTs beyond those campaigning on the issue. This raises the more general issue of whether an activist minority can override the views of a more passive majority.

The Campaign for Fairer Gambling, which leads the campaign against FOBTs, is funded by Derek Webb and Hannah O'Donnell. Webb was a successful poker player, businessman and the inventor of Three Card Poker, a game that is played worldwide on casino tables, and he is an expert in understanding gambling game content and gambler behaviour. He made £15m from selling his Prime Table Games business to the Las Vegas casino group Galaxy Gaming. Webb and his partner O'Donnell have retired from commercial activity following an asset sale of their gambling games to a US public company. Their parliamentary researcher was formerly addicted to FOBTs. The Campaign for Fairer Gambling does not want to prohibit FOBTs altogether, since this would be seen as too draconian and is not politically achievable. Their aim is to limit the maximum stake to £2. The industry could probably accept a reduction to £25. According to HSBC, 'if maximum stakes were cut to £10, machine revenues would drop by at least 30 per cent' (Ahmed, 2017: 19).

There is a snappily titled Fixed Odds Betting Terminals All-Party Parliamentary Group. This produced a report, which ABB complained was a front for commercial vested interests in the casino, arcade and pub industries. The backers of the report were eventually revealed as Bacta, the trade body for adult gaming centres and arcades; the Hippodrome Casino; Novomatic, a machine manufacturer for the casino and gaming industry; JD Wetherspoon, the pub operator, which has its own lower-stake gaming machines; LM Consulting, an arcades adviser; Praesepe, a casinos and arcades company; and the Campaign for Fairer Gambling.

In February 2017 the General Synod of the Church of England passed a motion calling for the maximum stake for FOBTs to be lowered to £2. The motion spoke of 'widespread public concern' over the large amounts being wagered on FOBTs in high street betting shops, and the 'destructive' impact of the machines on the lives of families and whole communities. Members also called on the government to bring forward proposals to amend existing legislation to grant local authorities the power to make provision regarding the number and location of FOBTs in order to reduce the risk of harm to vulnerable people. Other faith groups have taken an interest in the issue, such as Quaker Action on Alcohol and Drugs and the Evangelical Alliance.

The campaigning group 38 Degrees also became involved, dispatching teenage 'mystery shoppers' who were able to use FOBTs without being challenged in 65 out of 108 shops. The teenagers were all 18 but were chosen to take part because they looked younger. All the chains involved have policies to challenge gamblers who look younger than 21. 38 Degrees argued that ministers should cut the maximum stake and the speed of play.

The case against restrictions on FOBTs is formulated both in terms of the economic consequences and a view that the harm that is caused is exaggerated. A report commissioned from KPMG by the betting industry suggests that a significant cut to the maximum stake would lead to half of the 9,000 betting shops in the UK becoming unprofitable and at risk of closure by 2020. This would lead to the loss of 15,000–20,000 jobs. There would also be a knock-on hit to the racing industry of contributions of more than £100m from bookmakers in racing levies and media rights. It has been claimed that 'civil servants are briefing Prime Minister Theresa May about the effect the changes could have on horse racing. They believe her interest has grown following audiences with the Queen, a racing enthusiast' (Ahmed, 2017: 19).

The gambling industry argues that there is no evidence of a causal link between FOBTs and problem gambling; the use of FOBTs could be a symptom rather than a cause. A representative of William Hill drew the attention of the House of Commons Culture, Media and Sport Committee to 'the fact that there was no difference between the rate of problem gambling between the 2001 and 2009 British Gambling Prevalence Surveys (0.6% for both years), despite about 30,000 B2s being introduced between those surveys' (House of Commons Culture, Media and Sport Committee, 2012: 19). The committee noted the controversy, referring to the differing evidence it had received and suggesting that further research was needed.

In formal advice to the Secretary of State in 2013 on gambling-related harm, the Gambling Commission observed that machine gambling could be associated with particular risks for some people and that an individual does not need to be a problem gambler in a clinical sense in order to experience harm – a combination of high stakes and natural game volatility can generate very significant losses in a short space of time. It thought that the often cited figure of an £18,000 loss per hour on a B2 machine was 'astronomically improbable', but that losing (and winning) large amounts of money on B2 machines was 'well within the bounds of probability'. The Commission acknowledged that there was a 'serious case' to answer in relation to B2s but said that a precautionary reduction in stakes was 'unsupported by the available evidence' (Graf, 2013).

The Treasury has a considerable interest in the issue, as there is a 25 per tax on the profits from FOBTs (increased from 20 per cent in the 2014 budget). The industry certainly thought that it was worth talking to the Treasury. Between January and March 2017 the then Treasury minister Jane Ellison (who lost her seat in the 2017 general election) met with the ABB and the National Casino Forum, whose members make some money from FOBTs. The ABB also recruited as its director of industry and regulatory relations Dr Radomir Tylecote. He did not work directly for the Treasury, but was a member of the Behavioural

Insights Team, the 'nudge unit' that formed part of the Cabinet Office, which was then semi-privatised.

A fall in betting shop revenues from FOBTs could drastically reduce Treasury tax receipts from the machines, which raise around £400m a year. With the government facing pressure for less austerity, it is difficult to give up buoyant sources of tax revenue. This may help to explain reported tensions between the Treasury and the Department of Culture, Media and Sport (DCMS) over the issue in the summer of 2017. The Treasury was reported to be insisting that the DCMS find a way of replacing any lost revenues.

The views of the minister who was responsible for gambling, Tracey Crouch, were well known. While she was a backbencher she condemned the machines, and shortly after being made a minister she attempted to commence a review, only for it to be blocked by David Cameron and George Osborne. When Theresa May became prime minister, she gave Crouch the green light to review FOBTs. In October 2016 the DCMS announced a review of gaming machines and social responsibility measures to 'ensure that we have the right balance between a sector that can grow and contribute to the economy, and one that is socially responsible and doing all it can to protect consumers and communities'. The review included a 'close look' at B2 machines and the specific concerns about the harm they can cause (House of Commons Library, 2017: 3). The review was supposed to be published in the spring of 2017, but was delayed because of the general election. In October 2017 the government finally announced its intention to reduce the maximum stake on FOBTs, but stopped short of coming up with a definitive answer as to what the stake should be. Instead it launched a 12-week consultation on a range of options between £50 and £2, much to the disappointment of opponents of the machines.

The broader political context can have a profound effect on the outcome of a campaign. The best outcome in the 2017 general election for the betting industry would have been a strong Conservative majority. The Labour Party, the Liberal Democrats and the SNP all backed a reduction in the maximum stake to £2 in their election manifestos, showing what a high profile the issue had gained, with newspapers such as *The Times* highlighting it. The position of the Democratic Unionist Party (DUP) on the issue is particularly interesting and significant. FOBTs are operational in Northern Ireland, but the province is not covered by the 2005 legislation or the remit of the Gambling Commission. Instructing the DUP MP and FOBT critic Jim Shannon to postpone his Westminster Hall debate on FOBTs, the DUP leadership said that it wanted to make its voice heard to government on this issue. The view of those close to the industry was that 'The puritan edges of the industry will have a much stronger voice in deciding policy' (Gaming Business, 2017: 2). The government could rely on cross-party support from an anti-FOBT Parliament for reducing the maximum stake. The political climate does not favour an industry that 'finds itself under increasing political, media and regulatory pressure' (Gaming Business, 2017: 2).

The Green Belt

Green Belt policy was established in 1955, primarily to stop urban sprawl by keeping land permanently open; however, there is not necessarily a right of access there. Only a fifth of London's Green Belt has an environmental status or is open to the public as green space. It does not have any intrinsic amenity or aesthetic value, as do Areas of Outstanding Natural Beauty or National Parks. There are now 14 separate areas of Green Belt that cover 13 per cent of England, plus one in Wales; mostly open land and countryside around the largest or most historic towns and cities.

The policy came under increasing criticism after 2010 from economists, notably Nicholas Crafts. He pointed to the way in which economic recovery had been stimulated in the 1930s by private housebuilding at a time when there were few planning restrictions. Some of the features of this development attracted criticism, such as 'ribbon development' along roads and the relatively low density of development, which used up large amounts of land. These concerns led to a proposal for a metropolitan Green Belt around London in 1935. Crafts argued (2011: 28) that

> On grounds of economic efficiency, it is clear that a policy of liberalizing planning restrictions is highly desirable in any case and this could be an important complement to a policy to reduce real interest rates. House prices in the average district would be significantly lower and the housing stock higher.

He estimated that 'the equilibrium housing stock in England is at least 3 million bigger than at present and a transition from here to there could easily entail building 150,000 additional houses per year for quite some years with a direct impact on employment of around 750,000'.

One consequence of these interventions was that the Green Belt became a legitimate topic for public discussion, as part of an increasing focus on housing policy on the political agenda. It was no longer what has been described as a 'sacred cow' or a 'no go area in political debate' (Griffith and Jefferys, 2013: 33). Libertarian think tanks such as the Adam Smith Institute took up the issue. It was increasingly argued that housing development had been prevented or slowed down by local protest movements, often referred to as NIMBYs (Not in My Back Yard). Although they often framed their opposition in environmental terms, it was claimed that they were really concerned with protecting property values or retaining access to land use for recreational activities such as dog walking. Pressure grew for central government to change policy to facilitate more housing developments.

Among the strongest advocates of such a policy were, not surprisingly, the housebuilding firms, organised in the House Builders' Federation, which claims to represent 80 per cent of the sector. Individual large firms also intervened in the debate, with Persimmon calling in their 2017 annual report for a review of the Green Belt to boost housing. Housebuilders also received some support from the housing charity, Shelter. It argued that development on 1 per cent of reclassified Green Belt land would allow for almost half a million new homes. The Green Belt was crudely defined and included many areas of low-quality land in the same category as land with high environmental value.

The leading opponent of any erosion of the Green Belt was the CPRE, although it accepted that housing development could take place on suitable brownfield sites within the Green Belt. It has received support from other organisations such as the National Trust, Wildlife and Countryside Link, the RSPB, the Wildlife Trust, the Royal Town Planning Institute and the Open Spaces Society. The CPRE argued that the Green Belt is an asset for communities, a local countryside on their doorstep, with diverse local nature reserves, public footpaths and woodland. They also presented it as natural capital that helps protect high-risk areas from flooding, while plants, trees and grassland are great absorbers of carbon dioxide from the atmosphere, which helps combat the effects of climate change. Furthermore, the Green Belt was often good-quality agricultural land that could be used to grow and produce local food for nearby markets. The CPRE also argued that Green Belt developments were not making a significant contribution to the provision of affordable housing.

A number of apparently independent reports on Green Belt development appeared, which turned out to be funded by, or closely linked to, the same group of housing industry consultants. This reflected the momentum of a growing campaign from the housing industry for the Green Belt to be reduced in size or even scrapped. In 2015 there were three such reports and in 2016 there were five, compared with only a handful in the previous decade.

It comes as no surprise that an all-party parliamentary group became involved, the APPG for London's planning and built environment, which was set up in 2015. A report that it produced in October 2016 called for the 'modernisation' of the Green Belt to become a 'green web' laced with 'dense suburban development'. The report was co-authored by Jonathan Manns, who was director of planning at Colliers International, a planning consultancy used by many big housebuilders. The company co-funded the APPG report. Alice Roberts, the head of green space campaigns at the CPRE, commented on what she saw as 'essentially front operations for the industry'. She said: 'Developers have been extremely clever. They have managed to create the impression of a change of mood because the public and media see reports from reputable organisations and understandably think they are objective' (Gilligan, 2017: 2).

The National Planning Policy Framework (NPPF) introduced in 2012, which had a core presumption in favour of sustainable development, left established policy for Green Belts largely unchanged. However, Green Belt land was considered likely to be under greater threat than before as a result of the development and growth policies in the NPPF. Local authorities found themselves under increasing pressure to allocate more land for housing or face being stripped of their right to make local plans, which allow them to determine which areas should be developed. The government also offered councils financial incentives to plan for more housing under the New Homes Bonus scheme. The CPRE estimated that 'the Government will subsidise the proposed development in the Green Belt at around £2.44billion' (CPRE, 2017: 8). By 2017 a total of 425,000 houses were planned for Green Belt land. This was an increase of 54 per cent on March 2016, and the biggest year-on-year increase in building proposed in the Green Belt for two decades.

The May government placed a new emphasis on housing policy, which was related to the prime minister's concern about those who were 'just about managing'. However, she was pulled two ways on the issue. On the one hand, it was reported that the publication of a new White Paper had been delayed because it was not radical enough. However, May was also concerned about the possibility of a revolt by backbench MPs, reflecting 'Middle England' concerns about new housing developments. She also felt that she was personally in tune with 'Middle England', not least in her own constituency, Maidenhead, which was just the sort of area that would resist an erosion of the Green Belt.

When it appeared in February 2017, the White Paper, entitled

Fixing Our Broken Housing Market, stepped back from permitting building on Green Belt land. Not a single restriction on such building was lifted. A CPRE blog commented,

> we like to think we have had some influence on some of their thinking, especially the rowing back from a Green Belt free-for-all. In what looks like a positive result for CPRE, the paper includes a commitment to maintain strong protections for Green Belt — it emphasised again that Green Belt boundaries should only be amended in exceptional circumstances. (Thomson, 2017)

However, it was also emphasised that the threat had not passed and that the CPRE could not yet down tools. In its response to the government consultation on the White Paper, the CPRE was particularly concerned about the proposal to have five-yearly reviews of Green Belt boundaries conducted by local councils, which it felt undermined the permanence of the Green Belt.

The 2017 general election changed the political context of Green Belt policy. It was considered that one reason for the loss of Conservative support among 'millennials' was the difficulty they faced in getting on to the housing ladder. This could be seen as reinforcing arguments for building on Green Belt land. On the other hand, the government's narrow majority meant that it was vulnerable to any revolt by Conservative backbenchers on issues such as the future of the Green Belt.

The pro-development lobby was able to secure discussion of the principle and practice of Green Belt policy in a way that had not happened since it was initiated. However, the way in which this played out once again demonstrated the difficulty of changing an embedded policy that has strong lobbies protecting it. As far as public opinion is concerned, a 2010 national survey found a high level of awareness of the Green Belt. However,

> when questioned on potential development on the Green Belt, the survey results suggest that public views are variable ... The responses suggest that while there is public support for Green Belt policy, and that this strongly relates to its protective function, there is also the recognition that

>some development may be necessary. (CPRE/Natural
>England, 2010: 23)

Of course, respondents might take a different view if the Green
Belt land to be developed was near them. Such proposals usually
arouse strong local opposition.

More houses have been built on Green Belt land than in
the past, but housebuilders insist that this is still insufficient to
meet local housing requirements. The CPRE and the conservation lobby have been able to protect the principle of the Green
Belt, even if it has been eroded at the edges. The political costs
of fundamentally changing policy have so far proved to be too
great.

Conclusions

In the case of sugar, expert medical opinion helped to establish
the issue on the political agenda, building on the campaign relating to salt. There were multiple policy options available, so that
the government could pick and choose those it wanted to select,
which reduced the impact on the food industry. Governments
always like it if they can raise revenue from a substance that
is seen to have harmful effects, so it embraced the idea of a
sugar tax, but was less keen on restrictions on advertising and
marketing which would also affect the advertising and television
industries.

In the case of FOBTs, there was one simple policy solution that received support from a combination of moral and
commercial stakeholders, although the evidence for harm was
somewhat mixed and open to contention. Campaigners were
careful to avoid the option of prohibition, which would have run
up against arguments about freedom of choice. The campaign
seemed close to success by 2017 and had achieved this with
limited resources, although there was considerable media and
parliamentary interest. The political tide was running against
FOBTs even before the 2017 general election, which made an

outcome acceptable to the industry even more unlikely. The betting industry was encountering reputational problems, exemplified by the decision of the Football Association to cease having a betting partner, despite incurring a financial loss as a result.

Economists and the pro-development lobby helped to get the Green Belt on to the political agenda, changing its hitherto sacrosanct status. This was the issue where public opinion was clearly opposed to major changes, as reflected in the views of backbench MPs. The May government recognised a political imperative to build more houses so as to make housing more affordable. It was doubtful whether targets could be met by building on brownfield sites, although the CPRE pointed out that not many of those houses built on the Green Belt were affordable. The CPRE appeared to deploy a scattergun approach, mobilising any argument it could in favour of the Green Belt, although confusion about the purposes of the Green Belt made this approach tenable. Some erosion of the Green Belt occurred, but it was more limited than the housebuilders would have liked. Given concerns about 'millennials' getting on to the housing ladder, the issue remained on the political agenda.

In all these cases, business got far less than it wanted. The sugar industry was only partially successful in its rearguard action; the betting industry looked like suffering a commercial blow; and the Green Belt was largely protected despite the efforts of the development lobby. However, one needs to be cautious about the typicality of these cases. Two of the cases involved potential harm to health and well-being. The third involved a cherished asset that was linked to strongly held values about the countryside and Englishness more generally.

Nevertheless, some generalisations can be drawn from these case studies. Expert opinion can be significant, particularly where issues of public health are involved. Parliamentary opinion can be important, especially when there is a hung Parliament. Changes in the leadership of a government can lead to a new ordering of political priorities, as happened in the cases of sugar and housing. However, the 2017 hung Parliament placed new constraints on the government's freedom of action. Once again, with some lobbying activities, all was not as it seemed and there was a lack of transparency.

5

Regulating lobbying

SAMMY Finer (1966: 145) concluded his classic study of lobbying by stating that 'the lobbies become – as far as the general public is concerned – faceless, voiceless, unidentifiable; in brief, anonymous'. His final plea was for 'Light! More light!' Recent attempts to regulate lobbying have focused on securing transparency so that we know who is lobbying whom about what. 'Lobbying is best done, is most effective, when no one is watching' (Cave and Rowell, 2015: 1).

It is widely accepted that 'the work carried out by interest groups is a central and legitimate part of the democratic process within all liberal democratic systems' (Chari, Hogan and Murphy, 2010: 1). Concerns about lobbying cover both the process and the outcome. Does it involve dubious practices and/ or the illegitimate use of influence? There is concern that it can involve 'a selective approach to the truth, media manipulation, the undermining of opponents and other dubious practices' (Cave and Rowell, 2015: x).

It is not just business interests that are involved in such activities. In 2016 Friends of the Earth was forced to withdraw material about the impact of fracking for shale gas, after Britain's advertising regulator found that the claims made could not be backed up with evidence. The Advertising Standards Authority ruling related to a fundraising leaflet that said that fracking increased the risk of cancer and asthma for local residents and would cause water contamination, plummeting house prices and higher insurance bills. The Charity Commission dropped an investigation into the claims after the environmental group told the regulator they had been made by its non-charitable arm.

Does lobbying involve a bias in favour of particular interests, notably those of business? There is a lot of evidence to suggest that 'commercial interests dominate the influence business' (Cave and Rowell, 2015: 22). This book has looked at a number of examples involving the influence of the food industry in relation to public health issues.

> While representatives of the powerful food industry meet regularly with Defra officials and ministers, there is no comparable regular engagement with representatives of public health, consumer or environmental interest groups, and no evidence that considerations of public and environmental health are being taken into account by those planning for, and with responsibility negotiating over, Brexit. (Lang, Millstone and Marsden, 2017: 38)

However, the picture is a little more complicated than it might at first appear. Business does not always get what it wants because the terms of the debate can shift against it; the weight of evidence against an indefensible position can become too strong. However, this can take time and business is often able to water down proposals that are inimical to its interests.

Vogel (1989) argued that business influence on politics was cyclical, that it fluctuated over time and that business could find itself on the ideological and political defensive. The political reckoning of the 2008 financial crisis took a long time to arrive, but when it did business found itself in a difficult position, trying to cope with a populist wave. Brexit was something that very few businesses wanted. The influence exerted by business can be affected by the general political climate, which can change very quickly. When David Cameron was prime minister, the heads of Britain's biggest companies enjoyed regular meetings with him. His business advisory group, which met quarterly, was abolished by his successor, Theresa May. She launched her leadership bid with a speech equating business with executive greed and foreign takeovers. She presented herself as a champion of those who were 'just about managing' rather than a close friend to big business.

There were some signs of a thaw in relations before the 2017 general election, although it was still difficult to get face-to-face access to May. However, after the election, a new government advisory group involving the main business organisations was set up, headed by the chancellor, Philip Hammond, and with May expected to attend some meetings Policy shifted in the direction of an extended transitional deal with the EU after Brexit, which was closer to what business wanted.

The case for and against regulation

The case for the regulation of lobbyists is simple enough: it promotes transparency and accountability, and hence strengthens democracy. Whether by itself it can overcome biases in the lobbying system is another matter, but at least it can reveal what those biases are and subject lobbying to scrutiny.

The regulation of lobbyists, typically through a requirement to register accompanied by a code of conduct, has not gone unchallenged. A number of objections have been put forward. One is that of cost, but the cost need not be prohibitive, certainly in relation to the benefits obtained. It should also, in principle, be possible to recover the operating costs from registrants, although that has not happened in the UK so far.

It has been argued that a register could act as an entry barrier, discouraging citizen participation and directing activity towards commercial lobbyists. Much, of course, depends on how the registration system is constructed, and the UK register excludes many forms of lobbying, so it is hardly a major disincentive. An alternative argument is that a register confers legitimacy on the lobbying system, giving it a badge of recognition. This probably applies more to the voluntary registers constructed by professional associations of lobbyists.

It has also been suggested that increased transparency is not necessarily desirable and that 'in order to formulate "good policy", confidential negotiations are sometimes necessary' (Chari, Hogan and Murphy, 2010: 7). However, the content of any discussions is not necessarily revealed and the record of the lobbying that has taken place usually appears after the event.

The case in favour of some form of regulation of lobbying is overwhelming, while the objections that have been raised do not constitute an argument for failing to act. However, despite experience in various parts of the world, designing a system that is effective is not straightforward, and the UK arrangements remain a work in progress.

The UK system of regulating lobbying

In 2007 the House of Commons Public Administration Select Committee started an inquiry into the lobbying industry, the first investigation since one by the Select Committee on Members' Interests in 1991. In January 2009 it published a report calling for a statutory register of lobbying activity in the interests of greater transparency. In its response, the government reiterated the broader case for lobbying as a feature of democracy: 'Lobbying is essentially the activity of those in a democracy making representations to government on issues of concern. The Government is committed to protecting this right from improper use while at the same time seeking to avoid any unnecessary regulation or restriction' (Public Administration Select Committee, 2009: 2). The government took the view that widespread stakeholder engagement widened the evidence base and led to better decision-making. In any case, 'The Government believes that in the vast majority of cases, lobbying takes place in a legitimate and beneficial way' (Public Administration Select Committee, 2009: 2).

In March 2010 three former cabinet ministers were secretly recorded expressing an interest in working for a lobbying firm for a fee of £5,000. The Labour government then changed its position in favour of a statutory register of lobbyists, but nothing happened before the 2010 general election. The Coalition

Agreement of the Conservatives and Liberal Democrats included a commitment to introduce a statutory register of lobbyists and ensure greater transparency. In 2012 the Political and Constitutional Reform Committee published a report recommending that the proposal for a statutory register of 'third party' or commercial lobbyists be dropped in favour of a wider register of anyone lobbying professionally in a paid role.

The Transparency of Lobbying, Non-Party Campaigning and Trade Union Administration Act 2014 introduced a new registration system for consultant lobbyists which came into operation in March 2015. The post of Registrar was created on a part-time basis. The register was meant to be self-funding, with a registration fee of £950 in 2017. However, the budget for 2017–18 projected an expenditure of £276,000, but income of just £123,000. Initially, there were 115 registrants, and this had grown to 132 by June 2017. This compares with '1,300 in Ireland – which has a much smaller lobbying industry' (Cave, 2016: 1).

The Registrar has satisfied herself that 'evidence of unregistered consultant lobbying taking place is rare' (Registrar of Consultant Lobbyists, 2017: 4). Nevertheless, the working of the register has been widely criticised. It has been dismissed as a 'fake' (Cave and Rowell, 2015: 268) and 'completely unfit for purpose' (Cave, 2016: 1). Its main shortcoming is its limited scope. 'It cast a net so small and with holes so wide that the vast majority of lobbying will escape regulation' (Cave and Rowell, 2015: 270). The Association of Professional Political Consultants 'has estimated that the statutory register of consultant lobbyists covers only 1 per cent of those who engage in lobbying activity' (Transparency International UK, 2015: 14–15). The total number of lobbyists could amount to 4,000.

Because lobbying bodies consider the register too limited in scope they have established parallel registers. The Chartered Institute of Public Relations has established a voluntary register for all lobbyists, the UK lobbying register. Those on the register of the Association of Professional Political Consultants (APPC) are subject to a complaints and disciplinary process if they breach the APPC code of conduct.

Criticisms of the register focus on which lobbyists are included, the range of interactions that is covered and the impact of the legislation on existing activities by public interest organisations. The register only applies to lobbyists who are available for hire. Admittedly, their activities have been the subject of particular concern. However, there are far more lobbyists who work 'in house', not least for firms and business organisations, as well as those representing NGOs and trade unions. Indeed, some whose involvement in lobbying is marginal have been brought within the scope of the register, such as 'lawyers, accountants, management consultants and think tanks' (Registrar of Consultant Lobbyists, 2017: 2).

As for the range of interactions covered, 'lobbyists only have to name clients if they contact a minister on their behalf, even though lobbyists rarely meet with politicians on behalf of clients' (Cave, 2016: 1). Special advisors are not covered, even though they can be key persons of influence, particularly in terms of bringing an issue to the attention of ministers. Moreover, the rules 'do not cover interactions between lobbyists and mid-level civil servants, even though these officials can have a significant influence over how policy is developed within government' (Transparency International UK, 2015: 15).

The Registrar is not completely toothless, however. She initiated an investigation into the provision of support services to APPGs, of which there are over 550. They have been referred to a number of times in this book and there are concerns that lobbyists may offer secretarial facilities to the groups to gain back-door access to parliamentarians. The Registrar met Policy Connect, a company that is the secretariat for nine all-party groups covering issues such as health, manufacturing and skills and employment. Businesses who pay to become Policy Connect's members may attend events in Parliament which are attended by ministers. Private companies are asked to pay between £175 and £20,000 to become members of APPGs. Policy Connect insisted that it was a social enterprise providing a service for industry experts and ministers and the antidote to lobbying, but the Registrar found that Policy Connect should be defined as a lobbying company because it was paid money by clients who are then given the opportunity to meet ministers. Subsequently, the chairman of Policy Connect, Barry Sheerman, the MP for Huddersfield, had reluctantly to register as a lobbyist.

The legislation also regulates more closely election campaign spending by those not standing for election or registered as political parties. Under the Act, civil society organisations are required to register with the Electoral Commission if they plan to spend more than £20,000 in England or £100,000 in the rest of the UK. It has been claimed that this represents 'an assault on democracy in the form of the ability of charities and trade unions to campaign' (Cave and Rowell, 2015: 270). Greenpeace refused to register as an act of civil disobedience, arguing that the law neutered the power of campaigners to hold politicians to account while doing nothing to regulate actual lobbyists. It spent more than £125,000 on the 2015 election, campaigning against fracking and for fishermen to get a bigger share of fish quotas. It was fined £30,000 by the Electoral Commission for failing to register.

As it stands, the register is clearly inadequate. It needs to be widened to cover all types of lobbyists and meetings with mid-level civil servants and special advisors. Information needs to be provided on 'how much is being spent on lobbying; what policy, legislation or issues are being lobbied on; [and] whether or not they are employing anyone who has previously worked for the organizations or departments they are now trying to influence' (Transparency International UK, 2015: 4). In addition, it is surely inappropriate that MPs should be able to work as lobbyists. The chances of change occurring are not great, with the Conservatives and Liberal Democrats not mentioning the issue in their 2017 general election manifestos. The Labour Party promised to introduce a universal register and a statutory code of conduct.

Regulation in the EU

The European Parliament, which has always been a strong supporter of lobby transparency, initiated regulation for lobbyists in 1996 based around the issue of passes to the institution. In 2007 the European Commission approved a voluntary register for all those seeking to influence decisions taken in the European institutions. This register was launched in 2008. In 2011 a voluntary transparency register was launched covering the European Parliament and the European Commission, but not the Council. The objective was to identify which interests were being pursued, with whom and at what cost. There were 11,363 registrants in August 2017 (see Table 5.1).

The Transparency Initiative introduced in November 2014 required that all meetings between interest representatives and the Commissioners, their Cabinets and Commission director-generals must be published within two weeks of taking place. It did not cover meetings with Commission officials below

Table 5.1   Registrants on the EU Transparency Register by category, August 2017

Category	Number of registrants
In-house lobbyists and trade/business/ professional associations	5,619
NGOs	2,973
Professional consultancies/law firms/self-employed consultants	1,328
Think tanks, research and academic institutions	852
Local and regional governments and other public entities	544
Organisations representing churches and religious communities	50

Source: European Union 2017

director-general level who might be drafting policy and involved in its implementation. In the first year, the Commission published information on more than 6,000 meetings (approximately 5,500 for commissioners and 600 for director-generals). It was claimed that the introduction of this new system effectively made entry on the transparency register a mandatory requirement for anybody who wanted to meet the most senior EU decision-makers and officials. In 2016 the European Commission launched a consultation on the transparency register to gather stakeholder views on a future mandatory system for all EU institutions.

Pressure for greater transparency is maintained by the ALTER-EU coalition:

> The Alliance for Lobbying Transparency and Ethics Regulation (ALTER-EU) is a coalition of over 200 public interest groups and trade unions concerned with the increasing influence exerted by corporate lobbyists on the political agenda in Europe, the resulting loss of democracy in EU decision-making and the postponement, weakening, or blockage even, of urgently needed progress on social, environmental and consumer-protection reforms. (ALTER-EU, 2017)

The EU does provide funding for many civil society groups in order to offset the advantages enjoyed by corporate lobbyists. Environmental and climate-related groups have been funded through the LIFE regulation since 1992. Although most of the funding is for projects, operating grants are also provided. For example, in the financial years 2016 and 2017 the European Environmental Bureau received €1.4m and the WWF European Policy Programme €1.24m.

Conclusions: lobbying and the validity of democracy

Steps have been taken to create greater transparency around the activities of lobbyists, with more progress being made at the EU level. Organisations such as spinwatch in the UK and ALTER-EU monitor the progress that is being made and continue to agitate for further action. In the UK, the operations of APPGs remain a matter for concern. They are clearly very popular with parliamentarians, so reforming them may not be easy. However, people may be misled into thinking that their pronouncements and reports are as objective and authoritative as those of select committees, when in fact they have close links with particular interests whose claims they advance.

Is the democratic process unduly distorted by lobbying? Business does not always get its own way, even if it has a homogeneous position, which is often not the case. It has had to retreat on a number of issues, particularly those where there are public health concerns. The relative silence of business during the Brexit campaign suggested that it was inhibited by the danger of offending consumers; this was particularly the case for those businesses such as retailers that have a direct relationship with customers, who would be divided down the middle on the issue. Environmentalists have had some successes, for example in effectively stopping the commercial use of GM crops in Europe. However, some longer established groups such as the National Trust and the RSPCA have become targets for media campaigns on the basis of contested claims that they have misused their considerable power, for example in relation to hunting and prosecutions of individual animal owners in the case of the RSPCA.

There is no doubt that business has some crucial advantages. Its lobbying operations are very well resourced and highly sophisticated. Government relies on business to deliver economic success, which in turn has a considerable influence on its political fortunes. Business now faces a much more fragmented opposition than when it had to cope with powerful trade unions that were able to use the sanction of the strike. There is a real concern that the UK may become more like the USA, where business interests have penetrated far into the heart of the polity via campaign funding, although they have had to distance themselves from President Trump because of concerns about the reputational damage they might suffer from too close an association with someone who does not appear to subscribe to what up to now have been widely held values.

Public interest groups may be successful in getting issues on to the political agenda, but that is only one step towards meaningful change. Social media has made a difference, particularly in terms of reducing organisational costs, but it has been less transformative than is often claimed. Its instantaneous character and its ability to spread messages rapidly are out of sync with a much slower political process which requires sustained pressure to deliver change. Fracking is an interesting test case of whether environmentalists can actually stop something happening as distinct from imposing delays and increasing operational costs (including those of the police). Of course, it may turn out that oil and gas are not present in the UK in quantities or forms that can be commercially extracted.

Electoral politics can still trump pressure politics. For example, the changed political climate after the 2017 general election made the task of defenders of FOBTs more difficult. The Brexit referendum was a major defeat for business and the political establishment more generally, but a plebiscitary democracy might be seen as too high a price to pay for countering the influence of lobbyists. A more acceptable route may be to strengthen representative democracy by encouraging more citizen involvement in political parties and public interest organisations. Parliamentary scrutiny needs to continue to be strengthened and the misuse of the legislature checked. The activities of lobbyists need to be transparent and subject to enforceable codes of conduct.

The general issue of the validity, legitimacy and credibility of modern democracy raises much bigger issues than lobbying. Since the global financial crisis there has been a sense that the political class and the business class have become removed from the population, whose lot they do not really understand because they live in the 'Westminster bubble'. There is a perception that the divide between the haves and have-nots is widening and there has been a new focus on the ratios between the incomes of chief executive officers of companies (or universities) and their lowest paid employees, a cause taken up by Theresa May in what many regard as little more than a populist gesture. What is evident is that right-wing populism has acquired a new momentum in the United States and most European countries, although it has taken a more left-wing form in the UK.

Revitalising British democracy raises a whole range of issues such as electoral reform, the voting age, reform of the second chamber and the future development of the devolved administrations. However, lobbying is seen as something that reinforces the strength and exclusivity of the Westminster bubble and widens the distance between it and the everyday lives of the majority of citizens (or 'ordinary people' as they are sometimes patronisingly called). Even despite the growing strength of campaigning and public interest lobbies, there is a concern that lobbying serves the interests of the haves at the expense of the have-nots. Devices such as online petitions give the appearance of citizen engagement, but generally they deliver relatively little in terms of real change, although a petition on road pricing may have got government moves in that direction halted (though many think that road pricing would be an efficient way of checking traffic congestion and reducing environmental damage).

One of the paradoxes of this situation is that that much-derided polity, the EU, has perhaps done the most to systematically tackle biases in lobbying. It does seem to have had some real success in offsetting biases in stakeholder participation. The evidence and literature would seem to support 'an optimistic view over the democratic credentials and legitimacy of the EU consultation regime' (Bunea, 2017: 66). However, this is of little help to the UK, as whatever the nature of any transition arrangements, Britain is going to leave the EU in 2019. It will then run the risk of becoming a policy taker rather than a policy maker as far as the EU is concerned.

Leaving the EU does not, of course, rule out a domestic debate about lobbying, but there is little appetite for this among the political class. Politicians and civil servants may have half an eye on the future career opportunities offered by lobbying organisations as they enter a lightly regulated revolving door between government and the private sector. There is outside pressure for change, but it is not strong enough to bring it about on a sufficient scale. Hence, the reputation of contemporary democracy may be damaged by stories about lobbying, but that democracy is not vigorous enough to bring about needed change. This might seem a bleak prognosis, but the political context can change rapidly, particularly in a period when traditional voter loyalties are weakening or even disappearing. Advocates of reform should be patient and persistent, for their opportunity may come.

Further reading

Cave, T., and A. Rowell, *A Quiet Word: Lobbying, Crony Capitalism and Broken Politics in Britain* (London: Vintage, 2015) is a very readable book by two campaigning activists about the rise of commercial lobbying in Britain and the limited attempts to regulate it.

Chari, R., J. Hogan and G. Murphy, *Regulating Lobbying: A Global Comparison* (Manchester: Manchester University Press, 2010) looks at the regulation of lobbying across the globe, including in countries such as Canada and the United States, where there is a long history of efforts in this direction.

Crowson, N., M. Hilton and J. McKay (eds), *NGOs in Contemporary Britain* (Basingstoke: Palgrave Macmillan, 2009) offers case studies of the development of campaigning groups since 1945, including those related to women, sexual politics and drugs.

Grant, W., *Pressure Groups and British Politics* (Basingstoke: Macmillan, 2000) is dated, but it remains a comprehensive and widely cited analysis of pressure group activity in Britain.

Halpin, D., *The Organization of Political Interest Groups* (Abingdon: Routledge, 2014) argues that we have to take the question of how interest groups are organised seriously if we are to understand their role and their relationship to democracy.

Hilton, M., et al., *The Politics of Expertise: How NGOs Shaped Modern Britain* (Oxford: Oxford University Press, 2013) examines how NGOs have been affected by a changed political context and how they have changed politics.

Jordan, G., and W. Maloney, *Democracy and Interest Groups:*

Enhancing Participation? (Basingstoke: Palgrave Macmillan, 2007) critically assesses the contribution that interest groups make to the democratic involvement of citizens.

References

Action on Sugar (2017) 'Sugar and Health', http://www.actionon-sugar.org/Sugar%20and%20Health/150286.html, accessed 7 July 2017.

Ahmed, M. (2017) 'Bookies fear terminal decline from wager limits', *Financial Times*, 10 April, 19.

ALTER-EU (2017) https://www.alter-eu.org/who-we-are, accessed 8 August 2017.

APCO (2017) http://www.apcoworldwide.com/our-work/case-study/mars-food, accessed 30 May 2017.

Ashley, J. (2016) 'Theresa May's climbdown on obesity is her first big mistake', https://www.theguardian.com/commentisfree/2016/aug/19/theresa-may-climbdown-obesity-junk-food-industry-public-health, accessed 1 August 2017.

BBC (2013) 'History of political lobbying scandals', http://www.bbc.co.uk/news/uk-politics-22754297, accessed 30 August 2017.

Brooke, S. (2009) 'The sphere of sexual politics: the Abortion Law Reform Association, 1930s to 1960s', in N. Crowson, M. Hilton and J. McKay (eds), *NGOs in Contemporary Britain*, Basingstoke: Palgrave Macmillan, 77–94.

Bunea, A. (2017) 'Designing stakeholder consultations: reinforcing or alleviating bias in the European Union system of govern-ance', *European Journal of Political Research*, 56:1, 46–69

Burson-Marsteller (2017) http://www.burson-marsteller.co.uk/what-we-do/our-expertise/public-affairs/, accessed 30 May 2017.

Business Advisory Group (2017) https://www.gov.uk/government/publications/business-advisory-group/prime-ministers-business-advisory-group, accessed 12 April 2017.

Butler, D., A. Adonis and T. Travers (1994) *Failure in British Government: The Politics of the Poll Tax*, Oxford: Oxford University Press.

Cairney, P., and N. McGarvey (2013) *Scottish Politics*, 2nd edn, Basingstoke: Palgrave Macmillan.

Cann, V. (2016) 'Google: one of Brussels' most active lobbyists', https://lobbyfacts.eu/articles/12–12–2016/google-one-of-brussels%E2%80%99-most-active-lobbyists, accessed 1 August 2017.

Cave, T. (2016) 'Theresa May's chance to shine a light on lobbying', http://www.spinwatch.org/index.php/issues/lobbying/item/5893-theresa-may-s-chance-to-shine-a-light-on-lobbying, accessed 3 August 2017.

Cave, T., and A. Rowell (2015) *A Quiet Word: Lobbying, Crony Capitalism and Broken Politics in Britain*, London: Vintage.

Chadwick, A., and J. Dennis (2017) 'Social media, professional media and mobilisation in contemporary Britain: explaining the strengths and weaknesses of the citizens' movement 38 Degrees', *Political Studies*, 65:1, 42–60.

Chari, R., J. Hogan and G. Murphy (2010) *Regulating Lobbying: A Global Comparison*, Manchester: Manchester University Press.

Coen, D., and A. Katsaitis (2015) *Institutional and Constitutional Aspects of Special Interest Representation*, Brussels: Directorate General for Internal Policies.

Connect (2017) https://connectpa.co.uk/water/, accessed 1 June 2017.

Corporate European Observatory (2016a) 'Lobbying over croissants and coffee', https://corporateeurope.org/power-lobbies/2016/05/lobbying-over-croissants-and-coffee, accessed 1 August 2017.

Corporate European Observatory (2016b) *A Spoonful of Sugar: How the Food Lobby Fights Sugar Regulation in the EU*, Brussels: Corporate European Observatory.

CPRE (2017) *Green Belt Under Siege*, London: Campaign to Protect Rural England.

CPRE/Natural England (2010) *Green Belts: A Greener Future*, London: Campaign to Protect Rural England.

Crafts, N. (2011) *Delivering Growth While Reducing Deficits: Lessons from the 1930s*, London: Centre Forum.

Crouch, C. (2004) *Post-Democracy*, Cambridge: Polity.

Crouch, C. (2010) 'The global firm: the problem of the giant firm in global capitalism', in D. Coen, W. Grant and G. Wilson (eds), *The Oxford Handbook of Business and Government*, Oxford: Oxford University Press, 148–72.

Dommett, K., A. Hindmoor and M. Wood (2017) 'Who meets whom: access and lobbying during the coalition years', *The British Journal of Politics and International Relations*, 19:2, 389–407.

Edelman (2017) http://www.edelman.com/practice/public-affairs/, accessed 30 May 2017.

European Union (2017) http://ec.europa.eu/transparencyregister/public/homePage.do, accessed 8 August 2017.

Finer, S. (1966) *Anonymous Empire*, 2nd edn, London: Pall Mall Press.

Gaming Business (2017) 'Minority government worsens industry outlook on FOBT stakes', http://www.igamingbusiness.com/news/minority-government-worsens-industry-outlook-fobt-stakes, accessed 1 August 2017.

Gilligan, A. (2017) 'Lobbyists behind attack on green belt', *Sunday Times*, 5 February, 2.

GK Strategy (2017) https://gkstrategy.com/public-affairs/, accessed 30 May 2017.

Graf, P. (2013) Letter from Philip Graf, Chair of the Gambling Commission, to Maria Miller, Secretary of State for Culture, Media and Sport, dated 20 June 2013.

Grant, W. (1978) 'Insider groups, outsider groups and interest group strategies in Britain', University of Warwick Department of Politics Working Paper no. 19.

Grant, W. (2000) *Pressure Groups and British Politics*, Basingstoke: Macmillan.

Griffith, M., and P. Jefferys (2013) *Solutions for the Housing Shortage*, London: Shelter.

Hadfield, P. (2006) *Bar Wars*, Oxford: Oxford University Press.

Halpin, D. (2009) 'NGOs and democratisation: assessing internal variation in the practices of NGOs', in N. Crowson, M. Hilton and J. McKay (eds), *NGOs in Contemporary Britain: Non-state Actors in Society and Politics since 1945*, London: Palgrave Macmillan, 261–80.

Halpin, D. (2014) *The Organization of Political Interest Groups*, Abingdon: Routledge.

Hanover Communications (2017) http://www.hanovercomms. com/how-we-work/services/public-affairs/, accessed 30 May 2017.

Hansard (2017) 'Schools Update', Vol. 627, cols 563–87.

Hawkins, B., C. Holden and J. McCambridge (2012) 'Alcohol industry influence on UK alcohol policy: a new agenda for public health', *Critical Public Health*, 22:3, 297-305.

Hill and Knowlton (2017) http://www.hkstrategies.com/unit ed-kingdom/en-uk/our-expertise/#specialist-expertise-public-affairs, accessed 30 May 2017.

Hilton, M. et al. (2013) *The Politics of Expertise: How NGOs Shaped Modern Britain*, Oxford: Oxford University Press.

House of Commons Culture, Media and Sport Committee (2012) *The Gambling Act 2005: A Bet Worth Taking?*, HC 421 2012–13, London: House of Commons.

House of Commons Health Committee (2017) *Childhood Obesity: Follow-up*, 7th report of session 2016–17, London: House of Commons.

House of Commons Library (2017) *Fixed Odds Betting Terminals*, London: House of Commons Library.

Jordan, G., and W. Maloney (1996) 'How bumble bees fly: accounting for public interest participation', *Political Studies*, 44:4, 668–85.

Jordan, G., and W. Maloney (1997) *The Protest Business?*, Manchester: Manchester University Press.

Keating, V.C., and E. Thrandardottir (2017) 'NGOs, trust and the accountability agenda', *The British Journal of Politics and International Relations*, 19:1, 134–51.

Lang, T., E. Millstone and T. Marsden (2017) *A Food Brexit: Time to Get Real*, Falmer: University of Sussex Science Policy Research Unit.

Lent, A. (2012) 'The transformation of gay and lesbian politics in Britain', *The British Journal of Politics and International Relations*, 5:1, 24–49.

Liedong, T.A., and T. Rajwani (2017) 'Why Brexit will bring a boom in lobbying', https://theconversation.com/why-brexit-will-bring-a-boom-in-lobbying-76350, accessed 1 August 2017.

Lowe, P., et al. (1986) *Countryside Conflicts: The Politics of Farming, Forestry and Conservation*, Aldershot: Gower.

Lowe, P., J. Murdoch and A. Norton (2001) *Professionals and Volunteers in the Environmental Process*, Newcastle: Centre for Rural Economy.

Margetts, H., et al. (2016) *Political Turbulence: How Social Media Shape Collective Action*, Princeton, NJ: Princeton University Press.

McKay, J., and M. Hilton (2009) 'Introduction', in N. Crowson, M. Hilton and J. McKay (eds), *NGOs in Contemporary Britain*, Basingstoke: Palgrave Macmillan, 1–20.

Newington Communications (2017) http://newingtoncomms.co.uk/case-studies, accessed 30 May 2017.

Olson, M. (1965) *The Logic of Collective Action*, Cambridge, MA: Harvard University Press.

Olson, M. (1982) *The Rise and Decline of Nations*, New Haven, CT: Yale University Press.

Page, E.C. (1999) 'The insider/outsider distinction: an empirical investigation', *The British Journal of Politics and International Relations*, 1:2, 205–14.

Page, E.C., and B. Jenkins (2005) *Policy Bureaucracy*, Oxford: Oxford University Press.

Parker, G. (2017) 'May ensures only Brexit key allows entry', *Financial Times*, 12 April, 3.

Public Administration Select Committee (2009) *Lobbying: Access and Influence in Whitehall: Government Response to the Committee's First Report of Session 2008–09*, HC 108 2009–10, London: House of Commons.

Registrar of Consultant Lobbyists (2017) *Business Plan 2017–18*, http://registrarofconsultantlobbyists.org.uk/2017–2018-business-plan/, accessed 3 August 2017.

Remarkable Group (2017) https://remarkablegroup.co.uk/engagement/government-relations/, accessed 30 May 2017.

Rootes, C. (2009) 'Environmentalism', in N. Crowson, M. Hilton and J. McKay (eds), *NGOs in Contemporary Britain*, Basingstoke: Palgrave Macmillan, 201–21.

Rose, R. (1974) *Politics in England Today*, London: Faber and Faber.

Rutter, J., et al. (2017) *Better Budgets: Making Tax Policy Better*, London: Institute for Government.

Saunders, C. (2009) 'International aid and development', in N. Crowson, M. Hilton and J. McKay (eds), *NGOs in Contemporary Britain*, Basingstoke: Palgrave Macmillan, 38–58.

Smyth, C. (2017) 'Food giants reject lower sugar target', *The Times*, 22 March, 1–2.

Thom, B., et al. (2016) 'The Alcohol Health Alliance: the emergence of an advocacy coalition to stimulate policy change', *British Politics*, 11:3, 301–23.

Thomson, M. (2017) 'Housing White Paper: worth the wait?', https://www.cpre.org.uk/magazine/opinion/item/4512-housing-white-paper, accessed 2 August 2017.

Toke, D., and D. Marsh (2003) 'Policy networks and the GM crops issue: assessing the utility of a dialectical model of policy networks', *Public Administration*, 81:2, 229–51.

Transparency International UK (2015) *Accountable Influence: Bringing Lobbying Out of the Shadows*, London: Transparency International.

Truman, D. (1951) *The Governmental Process*, New York: Alfred A. Knopf.

Vogel, D. (1989) *Fluctuating Fortunes: The Political Power of Business in America*, New York: Basic Books.

Weber Shandwick (2017) http://webershandwick.co.uk/what-we-do/public-affairs/, accessed 30 May 2017.

Whiteley, P. (2012) *Political Participation in Britain*, Basingstoke: Palgrave Macmillan.

Index